WHAT EVERY ANGEL INVESTOR WANTS YOU TO KNOW

AN INSIDER REVEALS HOW TO GET SMART FUNDING FOR YOUR BILLION-DOLLAR IDEA

BRIAN S. COHEN

AND JOHN KADOR

NEW YORK   CHICAGO   SAN FRANCISCO
LISBON   LONDON   MADRID   MEXICO CITY   MILAN
NEW DELHI   SAN JUAN   SEOUL   SINGAPORE
SYDNEY   TORONTO

1 2 3 4 5 6 7 8 9 0   QFR/QFR   1 9 8 7 6 5 4 3

ISBN   978-0-07-180071-6
MHID   0-07-180071-9

e-ISBN   978-0-07-180072-3
e-MHID   0-07-180072-7

Library of Congress Cataloging-in-Publication Data
Cohen, Brian.
  What every angel investor wants you to know : an insider reveals how to get smart funding for your billion-dollar idea / by Brian Cohen and John Kador.
      pages cm
  Includes bibliographical references and index.
  ISBN-13: 978-0-07-180071-6 (alk. paper)
  ISBN-10: 0-07-180071-9 (alk. paper)
1. Capital investments. 2. Investments. 3. New business enterprises. I. Kador, John. II. Title.
  HG4028.C4C64   2013
  658.15'224—dc23
                                                                                        2013002312

McGraw-Hill Education books are available at special quantity discounts to use as premiums and sales promotions or for use in corporate training programs. To contact a representative, please e-mail us at bulksales@mcgraw-hill.com.

This book is printed on acid-free paper.

To my amazingly supportive family
and the New York startup community,
which nurtured my entrepreneur dreams
and now allows me to nurture those of others

Brian Cohen

To my son, Dan, who lives what
his father merely describes

John Kador

CONTENTS

FOREWORD

I first met Brian Cohen in a noisy auditorium at a business school competition at New York University. There were scores of investors and entrepreneurs, all trying to get their voices heard. It was hard not to be taken aback by Brian's desire to talk with every person in the room. What stood out to me was the fact that he treated everyone more like a long-lost relative rather than a potential investment or stepping stones on a path toward personal financial gain—he treated us like humans.

Starting a company is a journey into the unknown, especially for first-time entrepreneurs. In May 2008, I started this journey by leaving a job at Google to build a mobile app with my friend Paul Sciarra.

That initial app was called Tote, a collection of catalogs that you could browse on your phone. Tote had a few decent features, but none stood out as being great. We soon learned that in order to succeed, we needed to excel at one thing. Nearly two years later, in March 2010, Paul and I launched Pinterest along with our friend Evan Sharp. We focused on one core feature: the ability to collect in one place images that users found inspiring.

Four months later, we had only a few thousand people on the site compared to the millions that other successful consumer startups now see within weeks. Nevertheless, with Brian's guidance, we kept moving forward.

When Pinterest finally started growing, we realized that, for our first users, Pinterest was an extremely personal tool. People spend time on Pinterest planning the most important things in their lives, such as a wedding, the addition of new family members, or what furniture they will put in their homes. As we grew our team, we wanted to make sure we worked with people who understood what Pinterest meant to us and to our first users.

When the time came for Pinterest to raise money, we knew we wanted to find not just a financial backer but an angel investor who would also be able to help us navigate the journey on which we would embark. Advice from others indicated that the best angel investors are those who provide not just money but guidance, contacts, and wisdom—all backed by personal experience.

Brian is ever optimistic and has shown me the value of being a positive leader. At a time early in Pinterest's journey, he believed in what this very personal project of ours could be. He understood what Pinterest meant to our small team and what it could mean to millions of people. This book is full of advice on how to work with angel investors like Brian, but it's important to note that not every business deal will follow the same rubric. Every entrepreneur's journey is different, making it especially important to surround yourself with people who truly care for your cause.

Ben Silbermann
Cofounder and CEO
Pinterest
Palo Alto, CA

Introduction

THE CLOSEST THING TO SLAVERY

My path to angel investing began with a piece of unsolicited advice from my favorite professor while I was in graduate school at Boston University. Harold G. Buchbinder, or "Bucky," as he invited his students to call him, created the science communications program at Boston University.

I was just a kid from Brooklyn. I'm still not entirely sure why Bucky took an interest in me. I know he was intrigued by my organizing a dance marathon to raise money for muscular dystrophy and by how I was getting the university's administration to support it. I certainly didn't know the meaning of the word *mentoring*. But one day, Bucky asked me to stop by his office after class. "I think I need to share with you something that will make you more successful," Bucky said.

I was certainly intrigued. No one had ever spoken to me like that.

When I sat down in his office, he gazed at me intently and said, "Never, ever work for anybody. It's the closest thing to slavery."

I didn't understand what he was talking about. Everyone I knew in Brooklyn worked for someone else. I didn't even realize he was mentoring me. But his words must have settled somewhere deep within me, because when I graduated, all I wanted to do was start a company. Most of my friends went to work for media companies or educational institutions, and many of them have done very well. But for me, my path led to the very special version of freedom that entrepreneurialism makes possible. I thank Bucky every day.

To honor his memory, I established the Harold G. Buchbinder Entrepreneurial Business Competition, which gave BU College of Communication graduate students the opportunity to create, research, and develop a business plan supporting innovative products and services in media and communications. A $10,000 award went to the student judged to have the most innovative and compelling business plan. I call it inspiration money. Bucky's belief in me inspired me to go forward. My hope is that this gesture keeps alive the mentoring that Bucky so thoughtfully provided me, as well as many other students over the years. Want to know what the first winners did with their winnings and how their startup fared? See Chapter 6.

STARTUPS ARE A SOCIAL GOOD

This book starts with a basic premise: startups are good for society, and they need angel investors to help them get started and build a strong foundation. This book is a guide to bring entrepreneurs and angels investors together for their mutual benefit and for the benefit of the community.

I can't claim to be representative of any investor but myself. Every angel brings his or her own priorities, desires, and attitudes to the practice. I think there's room for almost every kind of mix, but I do ask that investors have the confidence to be up front about why they are investing and what values they represent. In that spirit, let me tell you why I am an angel investor and what perspective I represent.

I've asked hundreds of angels why they invest. Many invest for the financial return. Some do it for fun or to keep themselves engaged. Some are angels because they sincerely want to help entrepreneurs, although they are not necessarily good at it.

I've started a number of companies over the years. Some have been more successful than others, but all have shaped me as an entrepreneur, and I've learned valuable lessons from each. One of the most valuable benefits of starting companies is that I surrounded myself with lots of smart people. I hired perhaps a thousand of them over the years and developed a real kinship and camaraderie with many.

The entrepreneur identity became more central to my professional career and personal life and even shaped the way I parented my own children. Maybe I took it too far. I'll let you be the judge. As my children were growing up, I talked to them as if they were little entrepreneurs. As they got older, I actually said these words: "I expect each of you, before the age of 26, to start your own business." My children didn't have an immediate reaction. Maybe they never heard me. But their ears sure perked up after my next statement: "I'm not going to leave you any money, but I will invest in you."

I've told that story many times over the years, and I've noticed something funny. When some parents hear that statement—"I don't believe in leaving money to you, but I do believe in investing in you"—most of them stop short, their gaze settles at a point beyond the horizon, and they knowingly shake their heads as if I had articulated something important and true.

Other parents were not convinced. "Why are you putting your children under this pressure?" asked a friend with two preschoolers. "How do you know they want or even can be entrepreneurs?" I told him that the skills they would learn on the road to being an entrepreneur would make them more valuable to any employer.

In fact, sometimes I felt a little guilt-ridden because I might have been putting my children under too much pressure. The truth is, 26 was an arbitrary age that seemed impossibly remote when I first started talking to them about being entrepreneurs.

Much later, I began to formulate the answer to the question that earlier eluded me. Why was I so set on my children having an entrepreneurial identity? Here's the short answer: Entrepreneurial skills are always desirable. Even if you never run the company you start, even if you fail, I believe that everyone regards entrepreneurial leadership skills and experience as intrinsically desirable. People with entrepreneurial experience are simply more employable. So if my children want to work for Google or General Electric, I say that they will be in a far better position for having had an entrepreneurial experience. Employers value those people who have demonstrated a certain approach to leadership and getting things accomplished.

For years, I took a lot of grief from friends and family over my challenge to my children. But then something funny happened. The rest of the world caught up with me. Today, almost everyone wants to be an entrepreneur. High schools and universities are hotbeds for startups. Summer camps for ambitious children foster a rising spirit of entrepreneurialism. In disciplines, such as computer science and engineering, a majority of the best students are now working to start their own companies rather than pursuing traditional career paths at established organizations. Incubators and accelerators are popping up all over the world to nourish and cultivate the hunger of people to start their own companies.

Today, few people I meet are taken aback when they hear about my challenge to my children to start companies before they are 26. Incredibly, today, some people say, "Why wait so long?" The appeal of startups is so pervasive that my challenge now has become conventional wisdom, expected and unremarkable.

Three or four times a year, I get together for an informal dinner with a group of business executives. I look forward to the meetings because my thinking is always challenged, and I always learn something new. Recently, I suggested that all the executives invite their children. So the next meeting included not only the participants, but about 10 young adults all in their early-to-mid 20s.

It was fascinating to listen to these young people talk about what they were doing and thinking about doing. Most of them had good jobs at name-brand companies. I had invited my son, Trace, who had cofounded his first company, BrandYourself, while he was a sophomore at Syracuse University. He sold much of his interest in the company and is now my partner in a startup called Launch.it, which is based on the idea that all new products should be easy to find, discover, and share. I describe what became of BrandYourself in Chapter 3.

When it was Trace's turn to talk about himself, I felt a change of pressure in the room. The quality of attention from the group was different—more intense. After Trace finished, I turned to the other sons and daughters and took a chance. "Okay, guys, you just got to let me know something," I said. "I have a theory that none of you really want to stay in the jobs you have and that you'd rather be starting a company."

It was as if I had uncapped a bottle. As the conversation progressed, a key theme emerged. Almost without exception, the young adults expressed a real hunger, bordering on desperation, to launch a business. Many of them were already experimenting with ideas, taking baby steps on the road to entrepreneurialism. One was working on a lacrosse sporting site. Others said they were waiting for a "big idea" before they felt safe enough to leave the security of the corporate fold, even though they all admitted that security was an illusion. Many agreed that if by age 30 they still had not launched their own businesses, then on some level they would consider themselves failures.

It turns out that all the young adults really wanted to start their own companies. A few had practical ideas about the businesses they wanted to launch. Others were more tentative in their visions, but that didn't keep them from being highly enthusiastic about the outcome of a startup they would launch to success.

Some of them didn't seem to care what businesses they launched; they just wanted to launch a business. On one level it was nutty, but on another level it made perfect sense. As they talked about their dreams, it because obvious to me that they were talking less about launching businesses and more about taking control of their lives.

ENTREPRENEURIAL SPIRIT

This yearning to do a startup sometimes comes off as a spiritual quest, doesn't it? It's no accident the term to describe this yearning is entrepreneurial "spirit." On one level, it can be a bit much. Sometimes even my eyes glaze over from the earnestness of the pitches I hear. Yes, at the end of the day, a startup company, like angel investing itself, is just business. And yet, I'm here to tell you that there's something more to this entrepreneurial business than just business.

Every entrepreneur and most angels will agree that the entrepreneurial spirit isn't just about money. It's about creating relationships that serve as a force multiplier for the best that human intelligence can create. Entrepreneurial spirit builds wealth through resources that only the best relationships inspire. When it's done right, entrepreneurial spirit is about connecting dots that aren't yet visible. It's about having the intuition—the faith, if you will—to overcome every obstacle to cultivate innovation and initiative. The best entrepreneurs—think Steve Jobs—have this spirit in spades.

In 2005, Jobs gave the commencement speech at Stanford University. He was already aware of the diagnosis that would end his life just six years later. He told the graduates, "You can't connect the dots looking forward; you can only connect them looking backwards. So you have to trust that the dots will somehow connect in your future. You have to trust in something—your gut, destiny, life, karma, whatever. This approach has never let me down, and it has made all the difference in my life."

FOLLOW YOUR PASSION—OR NOT

A number of the kids at the dinner were confused by the passion thing. You know what I mean. According to the passion principle, all you have to do is to identify what you really like to do, what really gives you energy, and build a business around that.

It's a huge stumbling block. The ideal of developing a business concept through a passion-driven mentality is a false ideal.

To kids who have no clue what their passion is, the passion thing is confusing and adds unnecessary pressure. There's enough pressure associated with launching a startup; why add more? When I lecture at colleges and universities, I see students beating themselves up because they have not identified their passions. The quest often hurts a lot of kids because they feel stuck. Now not only do they feel the pressure of wanting to launch a startup, but they have to somehow identify their passion before they can launch it.

Is Passion Necessary?

Launching a startup does not require it be built around your passion. If you determine what your passion is, great! More power to you. There is one more variable to consider. But whether or not you find your passion, it may not necessarily point you to the best business to launch. Passion is an excellent guide for choosing hobbies but less so for choosing a business. Launching a business is about applying good business principles, finding what problems there are for disruption in the marketplace, applying innovative solutions, and—this may be the critical step—executing flawlessly. The quest for passion hurts students when it stops them from taking action simply because they are unsure of their passion. Some more pertinent questions are: Is there a need in the marketplace? Can I actually meet that need? What do I need to learn to implement those ideas into action?

Howard Morgan, a New York Angels investor and co-founder of First Round Capital, absolutely requires that the entrepreneurs he backs demonstrate both passion and the ability to communicate the Big Idea of the business. But passion alone is not enough. "I need to see that passion tempered by indisputable facts that the business is, in fact, a real business," Morgan says. "Show me how passionate you are about making the endeavor a profitable business."

Passion is surely a part of the equation. It's passion that will inspire your colleagues to work 20 hours a day to make the business successful, Morgan says: "Money comes from building something you love." But Morgan also wants the entrepreneur to articulate why the world not only wants the proposed product or service, but why the world *needs* it.

At this point, you may be wondering how my "start a business before you turn 26" challenge worked out for my children. I'd say pretty well so far. I already described how my son, Trace, founded a company while he was still an undergraduate, after having interned at another startup while he was in high school. That's what I mean by investing in my children.

My coauthor, John Kador, shares my commitment to independence. He started his career as a newspaper journalist and then became a technical writer for a software company. His last staff job was as a copywriter for a high-tech advertising and public relations agency in Washington, D.C. But, eventually John concluded that he would rather have independence than security. In 1984, the year his son, Dan, was born, he started Kador Communications, a company that offered a variety of editorial services, and was immediately successful. And it turns out he didn't give up much in the way of security. The companies that formerly employed him were all out of business before Dan was 10 years old.

I know Dan Kador, and his career trajectory seems to me typical of what more and more highly gifted young people want for themselves. Dan graduated in 2006 from the University of Illinois School of Engineering with a degree in computer science. He was recruited by some of the best companies in the country: IBM, Google, Lockheed Martin. He elected to take an offer from Salesforce.com, the smallest, youngest, and most entrepreneurial of the companies he was considering. In 2006, cloud-based computing was still in its infancy. Salesforce.com was known mainly for its customer relationship management (CRM) tools. Dan was attracted by the opportunity to have an impact on a growing company, which is really what entrepreneurs want most.

If Dan had graduated in 2012 instead of six years earlier, I'm convinced he would have been attracted to a startup immediately upon graduation. But at Salesforce.com, he was given an enormous amount of freedom. In 2011, Dan resigned from a very lucrative job, leaving option money on the table, to start his own business. With two buddies he has known since high school, Dan started Keen IO. Their business plan was accepted by TechStars, one of the premier high-tech accelerators. Today, the company has been fully funded. (Full disclosure: I am not an investor.) Three new employees now work side-by-side with the founders, and the first revenue customers have come on board.

SOME WORDS ABOUT THE BOOK

The title of the book—*What Every Angel Investor Wants You to Know*—is a bit misleading. A more accurate title would be, *What One Angel Investor Wants You to Know*. That angel investor, of course, is me. While I quote a number of angel investors, many of whom want you to know different things, and some of whom disagree with me, this book is really about my own perspectives on how entrepreneurs can get the most out their relationship with seed-round angel investors.

For that reason, the book is written in the first person. My coauthor, John Kador, agrees that the first person offers a level of intimacy and immediacy that the plural voice ("we" and "us") lacks. But the authors of this book do speak with one voice, so when you read "I" or "me" or "mine," think "we" and "us" and "ours."

A word about some of the descriptive terms angel investors use: I don't, for example, refer to entrepreneurs as "deals," as in, "Did I tell you about the incredible deal that walked into my office this morning?" Yes, I do deals, but I invest in people with names, and I like to keep the distinction clear. No founder wants to be thought of as a "deal."

When founders put their heads and hearts together for the sake of their startup, they are focused on one of the most important activities of their lives. Most think what they are doing is important and maybe even world-changing. Sometimes they're right. Founders would be offended to have me think of them as just deals—instruments for me to make a few bucks—and I wouldn't blame them.

Some entrepreneurs also talk about raising "smart money" and "dumb money." These are not terms that appeal to me. In Chapter 7 ("Investor Raising vs. Money Raising"), I present some alternate terms that I'd like to see replace the old phraseology.

The book is organized into 15 chapters. Each chapter concludes with a list of key takeaways as well as lists, exercises, quizzes, and other features designed to underscore the lessons of the chapter.

While the book is designed to be read from beginning to end, every chapter stands alone. You can start anywhere in the book and find value. It's probably just as useful if the chapters are read in reverse order. But in whatever order you engage with the ideas herein, I encourage you to remember that angel investing is a high-touch, personality-driven activity. For entrepreneurs pursuing seed money for a startup, the main lesson is to just be yourself.

The chapters are short enough to be read in one sitting, which means that in a week or so, you can be well on your way to being the kind of entrepreneur who accomplishes big things with angel funding. If you're willing to put in the time to prepare and show up as yourself, I believe this could be one of the most powerful and action-oriented books you've ever read. Good luck. I hope you succeed.

Angel Investing Is a Contact Sport

Listen up and warm up, entrepreneurs. You can be cool, but not distant. Success with angel investors requires more than just a great idea. It requires creating an emotional hugging relationship. Angel investing is truly a high-contact sport.

That's because you're not really raising money. If you do it right, you're raising investors who, like your family, need from the start to feel something warm and fuzzy—not just about your brilliant idea, but about you! I will describe the essential characteristics of investor raising in Chapter 7.

But for now, just be aware that there's a big difference between simply raising money and raising smart investors. That's the promise of this book. By the time you finish, you will know the techniques and have the emotional knowledge to get smart funding commitments sooner for your billion dollar idea.

My basic view of angel investing is that I'd rather back a good business that recognizes how to satisfy a customer than some ill-defined long-term vision. There's a clear difference between a good business and a good investment. The difference is always the entrepreneur. While I also expect a financial return, I believe that with the right leadership and great execution, the financial returns will come.

There are broadly two types of angel investors. There are those who make the limited occasional investment, and then there are those like myself, and many of my associates at the New York Angels, who invest together and speak with one voice. We're committed to the startup community we're serving. By investing in more startups, we develop better instincts to make the best investments.

Founders have a tendency to think that all money is the same. That's not true. Money attached to an angel who is prepared to stick with you over the long haul, and is in a position to get you even more money, is infinitely better than an isolated check that has a number of zeros with no real number in front. You see, it's not the money that's really doing the heavy lifting for your startup; it's your choice of the smart angels who are investing in you, not just your company. They want to feel an emotional connection—in some sense, bragging rights that they found you first.

Angels really resonate with entrepreneurs who focus on choosing the right investor before the money. The other day I sat down with a founder I had just met, and I asked him what business he was developing. His reply startled me.

"It's the travel business you just invested in," the founder said.

"Wait, I invested in your business?" I was momentarily confused.

"No," he said. "You invested in my competitor's business."

Of course. I had recently invested in a travel business, and the founder knew that. And my response was, Wow, I'm impressed that I'm being tracked by this guy. "How did you know about my investment?" I asked.

"Nothing was easier," he said. He studied the New York Angels website, its profile on Gust, AngelList, and TechCrunch (see Chapter 10) and basically talked to everyone who crossed his path. The angel community is a small world. He did his homework. Now, I was pretty much locked out of investing in his company by virtue of my commitment to his competitor, but I'd be lying if I said I didn't have a twinge of regret that he didn't get to me first.

Here's a little secret many startups eventually learn for themselves: angel investors are generally less valuable for the wisdom of our advice (though it comes in handy from time to time) than for our contacts and introductions to people who can be really useful as the business develops.

YOU CAN'T BE SUCCESSFUL AT A DISTANCE

Let me say it another way, and this time I'm talking to both entrepreneurs and investors: you can't be successful at early-stage investing at a distance. The founder and the angel need to stay close, and not just during the courtship phase of the relationship. The mentorship that founders so desire and the mentorship angels are willing to offer really defines a mutually beneficial relationship.

Gabriel Weinberg, a Philadelphia-based angel investor and CEO of the search engine DuckDuckGo, learned this lesson after investing in 10 startups. Initially, one of his investing practices was to be location-agnostic. He felt that with the Internet, the physical location of the founders was irrelevant. After three years, he came to see this assumption was a mistake, concluding that it's much better to invest in startups that are near his base, the better to provide mentoring, support, and overall contact.

By contact, I mean that the angel spends significant time with the founder(s) and their team. The angel must really engage with the world that the team is in. The angel has to appreciate this world in a visceral way, not only for the benefit of the investment du jour, but to help sharpen the angel's instincts for emerging opportunities. It could be regular face-to-face contact with ongoing phone calls in the early stages of the business. In the end, it's up to the entrepreneur to determine the need and frequency of contact.

KNOW WHAT YOU'RE GETTING INTO

I'm always glad to support the dreams of entrepreneurs by offering my experience, mentorship, and financial investment. All I ask is that you be absolutely sure that you are interested in raising money. Because if you're not sure, the process will only create mayhem for you. Raising money from angel investors can be a lengthy, maddening, and often disheartening process. So be careful what you wish for because you might get it.

That's when—assuming you are successful in raising sufficient investment to fund a company—the excruciating fun begins. You will then find yourself in partnership with investors who effectively own a piece of your life. They will have opinions, rights, and the standing to question decisions you make. Perhaps, even more important, you will have a fiduciary responsibility to them, which means that you can't simply wake up one day and say, "Guess what? I'm bored with all this, so I'm just going to try something else for a while." Instead, your only exit strategy will be to make the startup such a success that another company will eventually come along and buy it for a lot of cash. Until then, be prepared to exist with unrelenting pressure and frustration. So, do you really want the money?

YOU ARE IN CONTROL

I want entrepreneurs to know they are in control and act like it.

Control is not the first thing that most first-time entrepreneurs believe they have. So when I speak at colleges or business schools, I usually start by getting my audience to consider that they really are in control. I've been known to address a group of entrepreneurs by asking them to repeat these words after me: "I am in control." By the giggles and embarrassed looks, I can see that this message does not go down naturally.

There's nothing more powerful or attractive to a smart angel investor than entrepreneurs who own the idea, own the execution, and recognize the tools and resources they need to succeed. They don't just look to achieve success; they see success as inevitable. They are more focused on what they have already created than what they still need. This ownership is what I mean by control. I believe that sense of ownership and control should be complete and absolute.

You are in control. If there's only one insight you take away from this book, I ask that it be this: you are in control. This book is really a road map to show you how to be in control. The sooner you accept that reality, the sooner you can leverage the control you have to move your startup forward.

Too many entrepreneurs give away control, and too many angels are willing to let them do it. It's tempting for angels to invoke the Golden Rule—"he who has the gold makes the rules"—and thereby cop an attitude that angels have all the power and the founders have none. This attitude is not only plain wrong but counterproductive, as smart angels soon discover.

In fact, it's the entrepreneur who has the power and control, and the sooner both parties recognize this, the better. Nothing happens until you make it happen. You do all the heavy lifting. You're going to develop the product, hire the talent, call on customers, and run the business. Angels merely enable the process. I emphasize the issue of control whenever I interact with entrepreneurs because it so central to initial and subsequent funding.

The world has changed. You have been empowered in important new ways, and it's essential that you seize your power. It takes nothing from me when you do seize power, and, in fact, it benefits me in the long run. That's because when you are in the driver's seat, you know better what you are doing and have a plan where this level of control is in the service of ownership. I like to get founders to incorporate a stake in ownership and control as soon as possible. I want you to own the process, the success if it comes, and the failure if it doesn't. I have seen that accepting ownership early forces entrepreneurs to be smarter about the questions they ask, more disciplined about how they apply the answers, and less tolerant of wasting time. It leads to better outcomes for all concerned.

One better outcome: more pointed questions for me. That forces me to up my game. When founders are in touch with their control, it also saves time.

Why is it that when it comes to term sheets, founders are content to wait for whatever angel investors deign to provide? Terms sheets are not written in stone like tablets from on high. I actually like it when entrepreneurs help drive the process by outlining their own term sheets up front without waiting for me. I'm absolutely fascinated to see what they think the valuation and other terms should be. It's a revealing exercise to see what a team's expectations are and where the line starts. It's like the entrepreneur is saying to the angel investor, "Hey, I have some responsibility and control here. It's not just a one-way street. Let me tell you where I think we can start." Of course, it doesn't always mean I'll immediately agree with the numbers. But I know it speeds up the process, because now I'm much clearer about expectations, and we have something specific to talk about at the outset of negotiations.

For me, this is just sound business. But I must warn founders that some angels might still be taken aback by such chutzpah. Then again, such investors would likely prove to be weak investment partners, anyway.

ANGELS TO AVOID

Some angels don't fly as high as others. Be wary of unscrupulous characters posing as angel investors. Here are some of the more common varieties.

- **Shark angels.** Be leery of angel investors who want to take. Angels should be givers, not takers. Investors who ask you for a job are thinking only of themselves. Stay away from them.

- **Angel brokers.** Brokers will ask startups to sign a fee agreement for introductions to actual investors. Some brokers may provide a needed service, but I advise you stay away from them. Frankly, with the online tools available today (some of which I describe in Chapter 10), startups should be able to find angels. Demonstrating that ability goes a long way, in my mind, to showing me that the founders are smart and disciplined. In any case, I won't invest in you if you've used an angel broker. I want my money to fund your intellectual work. It's distasteful to see a portion of my investment go into a broker's pocket.

- **Controlling angels.** Angel investing seems to attract a number of formerly successful businesspeople who think they are smarter than you. They are usually overbearing and hypercritical of every decision you make. Don't be intimidated into bad decisions.

FOUR ATTRIBUTES OF FUNDABLE STARTUPS

Fundable startups need four attributes to impress angel investors. They have to have a capacity for growth and be scalable, profitable, and sustainable. If you have a startup that has all four of these attributes and you can demonstrate that you have a reasonable shot of not totally screwing up the execution, most angels will beat down your door to write you a check.

Capacity for growth means simply that the business has what it takes to keep growing. A lot of startups that come to me can't pass this test. Usually it's because there's a lot of confusion about what's a product and what's a company. I often see awesome ideas and a great solution. But what I have to tell the founder is, "What we have here is really a product, not a company."

Scalability is related to growth. A scalable startup is one that starts with a business model that can take an innovative idea and, by leveraging the power of technology, achieve essentially unlimited orders of magnitude of productivity. Expedia and Twitter are examples of scalable businesses because the costs of serving one million or 100 million customers are essentially equal. In contrast, there are many fine and profitable businesses—restaurants, dry cleaners, hairdressers—that are not fundable because they don't scale well. A hairdresser can serve only a fixed number of clients per day, and there is little technology can do to alter that fact.

That said, scaling is very difficult. A lot of highfliers such as Groupon and Zynga still can't quite get the formula right. Transforming startups from baseline to sustainable, scalable, profitable business models takes inordinate work and not a bit of luck.

Profitable means that revenues exceed operating costs.

Sustainable means that profitability will be ongoing for the next period, and there are no obvious obstacles to that condition. The most experienced angels have learned that the best startups to invest in feature high technical risk and low market risk. Technical risk imposes costs on startups; market risk causes startups to fail. In other words, smart angels look for startups that are highly likely to succeed if they can really deliver on their technical promises.

The problem is that the Internet startups that most angels like to invest in feature the reverse pattern: they usually have low technical risk and high market risk. That is, there is usually very little risk that these startups can't deliver their product. The chief issue is whether the startup's product is of value to a large enough customer base that the startup can acquire at affordable costs.

EXCITING TIME

It's an exciting time to be an entrepreneur. Two global forces are intersecting to facilitate the creation of new businesses. First, innovation has never been easier, faster, or cheaper. Second, the pool of wealthy people has gotten larger, injecting an ever-growing group of relatively young, curious investors looking for thrill-seeking opportunities to help build new businesses and further expand their own wealth. This combination represents a perfect storm for savvy entrepreneurs.

It's not bad for savvy angel investors, either. There's something compelling about the fact that many of the people who have most benefitted from the economic gains of the past decade—think about the young millionaires of Google, PayPal, and Facebook—are the ones funding the prospects of the next generation.

Historically, innovation has been an expensive slog. Thomas Edison required more than three years, a large team of researchers, and 3,000 discrete experiments before he refined the incandescent light bulb in 1879. James Dyson developed a very powerful bagless vacuum cleaner, but it took him over 200 prototypes and five years. The development of Mosaic, the web browser credited with popularizing the World Wide Web, took over a year. Both development efforts required huge investments in time and capital. Innovation progresses, as always, by trial and error, but when trial cycles require a great deal of time and money, innovation pays the price.

Today, thanks to developments in open-source tools and cloud-based infrastructure, the cost of trial cycles is approaching zero. Startups that formerly required millions of dollars in capital can now be built quickly, sometimes in hours, by small groups of highly productive teams using digital tools for very manageable sums. As the cost of innovation decreases, so does risk, which, in turn, increases the pool of capital available to finance the next round of ever-cheaper innovation, unleashing new waves of human potential and creating another generation of high-wealth individuals who, in their own turn, will help co-create another cycle of innovation and prosperity. Now that's what I call a virtuous cycle.

Innovation and access to capital represent an explosive combination, but there's yet another factor that makes this period of innovation so powerful for smart entrepreneurs. We all know the digital revolution is exploding. Facebook now has more than one billion users. If Facebook were a nation, it would be the third most populous nation in the world. There will be more cell phones than people in the world by 2016, according to Cisco Systems. Mobile tablet sales are outpacing PC shipments. Increasingly, we are seeing a massive addressable audience for digital innovation. The operative word here is "addressable." It's a word that angel investors love because it means startups have a good shot at actually defining and capturing a market.

The cost of attempting digital innovation has never been lower, the pool of capital available to fund innovation has never been larger, and the economic value of a "winning" digital innovation has never been greater. No wonder the market for "disruptive" digital innovation is blowing up.

The current surge of entrepreneurs will create many viable businesses, with happy customers and growing revenues. But only a tiny sliver of them will strike the magical balance of talent, insight, effort, and luck that produces fundable startups. Angel investors all over the world are hoping that your startup will be the exception. The following pages represent a road map for entrepreneurs to position their startups to get the best from angels and for angels to get the best from entrepreneurs. When that happens, everyone's the winner. Let's get started.

CHAPTER 1 TAKEAWAYS

- Successful angel investing requires intimacy.

- All money is not the same.

- You are in control.

- It's your choice of angels—not the money—that's doing the heavy lifting for your startup.

- Fundable startups need scalability, growth, profitability, and sustainability.

Early Stage Investing and Why Angels Are Your New Best Friend

2

Early-stage investors come in many forms. But most entrepreneurs look to three basic types of investors when they need seed-level financing: friends and family, angel investors, and venture capitalists (VCs). A few prepared and lucky entrepreneurs have the resources to bootstrap their startups—that is, using their own money—but almost all startups need outside funding to build their core teams, develop their minimum viable product, and find their first customers.

An angel investor is an individual who, using his or her own money, provides early stage startup capital to a new business and expects a percentage of ownership equity in return with the expectation of a sale or "exit."

In the United States, the term "angel" comes from the Broadway theater scene, in which investments by wealthy sponsors made lavish theatrical productions possible. Like today's angels, these high-wealth individuals were looking for a little excitement in their lives as well as a return. Theater angels, like their modern counterparts, thought they were good at spotting new talent or recognizing the merit of intellectual property such as scripts and musical scores. Such investors often swooped in from lofty heights to save the show at the last minute. Hence they were dubbed "theater angels."

Less is known about angel investing than venture capital because of the private nature of the investments. However, almost every major business success story can trace its initial entry into the market to one or more angel investors who took the biggest risks and provided the needed knowledge, contacts, and certainly capital to help the company achieve its fast growth trajectory.

According to the U.S. Small Business Administration, there are about 250,000 active angels in the United States, funding about 50,000 startups a year. Angel investors annually commit about $20 billion to startups, with friends & family members funneling another $50 to $75 billion into more than 200,000 companies. There are over two million people in the United States with sufficient discretionary net worth to make angel investments. With every IPO such as Facebook, new angels are generated. Substantial angel and VC activity takes place in Europe, South America, and, increasingly, Asia.

WHY I'M AN ANGEL INVESTOR

You may be wondering why I am an angel investor. What's in it for me?

A return on my financial investment is certainly one reason, but it's much lower down the list of reasons of why I invest than many entrepreneurs might suspect. And based on the hundreds of angel investors I work with, I don't believe my priorities are an exception.

I can't imagine a better thing to do at this stage in my life. I believe that it's a privilege to be an angel investor working at the disruptive edge of ideas that could change the world. I believe that entrepreneurialism is the embodiment of creating a newer, better world for my children. When people ask me about my faith, I reply that I believe in the entrepreneurial spirit.

The other day, I appeared on *Your Business*, the MSNBC program hosted by J. J. Ramberg. I was on a panel of angel investors. Ramberg asked each of us to identify our political affiliations. One noted he supported the Republican Party; the other said he was a Democrat. They looked at me and I said, "Oh, I'm from the Entrepreneurial Party."

The biggest driver for me is the thrill of inspiring, advising, and mentoring the brightest young minds in the world as they work incredibly hard to create something new and exciting. The chance to improve the world is what gets me up in the morning with a checkbook in my breast pocket.

I'm fascinated to have a front-row seat at the development of what I hope will emerge as the next Google, Twitter, or Pinterest, all of which were, at one time, little more than gleams in the eyes of very smart founders supported by very lucky angel investors. None could know with certainty that they held anything of value. I want my world to explode by being the first to see highly disruptive technologies where, if the founder gets it even half right, there's an opportunity to make a difference in improving the world.

Starting a business by raising early stage capital is hard, frequently disheartening work. I want to help. Being a good listener is the first step. Entrepreneurs need someone to listen to and, in the end, someone to listen to them. I'd like to be available at both ends of the process.

Although I've been a full-time angel investor for six years or so, the core of my career has always been about startups. At TSI, the public relations firm my wife and I built into one of the largest high-tech PR firms in the country, many of the clients I took on were just starting out. Even when we represented established clients such as IBM or Sony, they tended to be entrepreneurial driven companies constantly launching new initiatives and products.

In fact, my first investment as an angel investor was in a TSI client called Multiflow Computers, Inc. Founded in 1984, Multiflow was a New Haven, Connecticut–based manufacturer of a minisupercomputer called the Trace 7/200. As a business, Multiflow had a short life, even though the technology it spawned had an outsized influence on the future of the computer industry before the company went bankrupt in 1990. As an investment, it was a total bust, and I lost everything. But the experiment wasn't a total disaster. My oldest son's name is Trace.

Another reason I am an angel is that my angel investor colleagues are some of the finest people I have ever met. My fellow New York Angels are now among my closest friends. I love how networking with other angels spawns smarter investments, more collegial relationships, and better-performing startups.

I come at angel investing with a great sense of optimism, all financial evidence to the contrary. It's very hard for an angel investor to make money. At this writing, after six years and investments in dozens of startups, my portfolio is looking very good. Certainly as the first angel investor in Pinterest, I am in a very fortunate position. Thanks to Pinterest's incredible success, I may see my initial investment multiplied by a thousand or more. That will allow me to broaden my angel investing activities even more.

In Pinterest, I saw an opportunity for a new brand of social media. I also glimpsed something exciting in cofounder Ben Silbermann, and I decided to invest in him long before the virtual bulletin board the world now knows as Pinterest took shape. But I don't want to kid you. Luck goes a long way. It's also true that angels make their own luck by meeting as many entrepreneurs and seeing as many pitches as possible. It helps to be a startup junkie.

I push every member of the New York Angels to get as much education in every aspect of startup dynamics as possible. If you lean into the work as much as I have, you, too, can be a much more successful investor.

DO ANGEL INVESTORS MAKE MONEY?

The short answer, for the great majority of angels, is no. Even the smartest angels I know feel lucky if they are net-zero after a few years. I personally don't know more than a handful of angels who had decent exits. The reality is that most startups fail, and despite what angels may believe about their ability to distinguish the winners from the losers, most angels, including me, aren't that smart.

It's impossible to get verifiable statistics on the financial returns of angel investors in the tech sector. According to a recent report from the Kaufmann Foundation, in the VC industry, which is much more transparent, the average fund formed during the past decade barely returned its investors' capital after fees.

If the average VC fund barely makes money, and early stage seed investments represent even riskier opportunities than the ones pursued by venture capital firms, then the typical return for angels can't be much better.

Nevertheless, all angels think they are like the residents of Garrison Keillor's Lake Wobegon, where all the children are above average. Improbably, every angel regards their own instincts as just a little better than their peers. But just as half of all doctors graduated in the bottom half of their medical schools, 50 percent of all angels are working at a deficit.

It's crucial to regard angel investing as a money-making business. Returns from earlier opportunities make it possible for me to continue investing. Most angels wouldn't mind making a few smaller hits along the way—anything from multiples of 2X and up—if they see the opportunity to make a difference. Like most investors, I'm interested in steady returns and the occasional big hit. Okay, I'll fess up. If I'm candid about it, that's the business all angels are really in—the hit business—even though many angels go through their entire investment careers without seeing a single big score.

But hey, as an accredited investor, it's money that I can afford to lose. A clear-headed appreciation of the risks backed up by a minimum level of wealth is one of the key requirements of being an angel. Yes, angel investing is like gambling. But the odds at roulette, frankly, are better. So if the odds were the only thing that mattered to me, you'd find me in Las Vegas. But you won't find me in Vegas, except in January at the Consumer Electronics Show. I choose to be in New York City, because something exciting is going on here, and I get to be a part of it. So until roulette can be a force multiplier for human capital and as powerful an impulse for social change as helping the world's smartest entrepreneurs make the world just a little better, I'll stick to angel investing and take my chances.

The purpose of accreditation is manage risk: to minimize the possibilities for investors to lose more money than they can afford to lose. To become an accredited angel investor, you must be deemed to have sufficient financial sophistication and wealth to make risky investments. It's hard to measure sophistication, so regulators assume that if an investor amasses sufficient wealth or has a sufficiently high income, that's good enough. Currently, in order to be accredited, angels must meet any one of three conditions: assets of at least $1 million (not including the value of the primary residence); annual income exceeding $200,000 in each of the two most recent years; or joint income with a spouse exceeding $300,000 for those years, with a reasonable expectation of at least the same income level in the current year. Less than three percent of Americans can meet these conditions.

Now, there are plenty of people who invest in early stage companies who are not accredited, and there is no legal requirement for entrepreneurs to work only with accredited investors. However, while you can raise money from nonaccredited investors, securities regulations require significant additional disclosures and documentation designed to protect both the investor and the entrepreneur. Trust me, you'll go blind filling out all those extra forms. For that reason, most entrepreneurs wisely restrict their appeals to accredited investors, and that's why the New York Angels requires evidence of accreditation of its members.

ANGELS AT WORK

Many angels work individually, investing in as few as one opportunity per year; some super angels invest in up to 20 or more startups per year. Today, successful angel investors also form syndicates or angel networks where several investors combine their capital in an attempt to impose discipline on the process and benefit from economies of scale.

When I started, the angel investment landscape was limited to undisciplined elites. Funding activities were usually made on the basis of personal relationships and friends of friends, legitimately criticized as "the old boy's network." Funding was based on who you knew, not necessarily on how well the angel fit the investment. In any case, the tools to determine the soundness of an investment opportunity were relatively immature. In the last 10 years, however, the angel investing market has become much more transparent, inclusive, and rigorous. The process has been aided tremendously with deal and investor relations management platforms such as Gust. (See Chapter 10 for more on Gust, AngelList, and other collaborative tools for entrepreneurs.)

Angel Groups

Angel networks, emerging in the late 1980s, were formed when individual angel investors came together in syndicates to pool their resources (capital and expertise) in order to participate in a larger number of investments and minimize risk by diversifying. Today, these angel groups comprise anywhere between 10 to 200 members, each with a common interest of using personal funds for joint investments. In 2012, there were over 340 major angel groups in the United States, up 13 percent since 2011, according to Angel Capital Education Foundation reports. Over 800 angel groups around the world are connected through Gust.

The rise of angel groups makes life easier both for angels and for founders. These angel groups provide needed education, training, and mentoring for angels. I've found that the angels' camaraderie and social relationships create a dramatically smarter investment environment. That draws more people into angel investing, which is good for startups. More angel groups are organizing events where they can hear pitches from entrepreneurs. Some angel groups are organized around industries such as nanotechnology, life sciences, or social media, giving entrepreneurs a better shot at connecting with the most receptive angels.

While some groups charge a fee for founders to make pitches, I don't think entrepreneurs should be asked to pay anything. The angel investors are certainly rich enough and smart enough to get sponsors to offset any administrative costs.

The New York Angels is a typical example of an angel group. A member-led organization committed to finding, funding, and mentoring great young companies from pitch through a successful exit, the New York Angels has been the leading seed investment organization in New York City for over a decade, since its founding in 2003 by some of the City's most active angels, including David S. Rose, Howard Morgan, Josh Kopelman, Esther Dyson and Scott Kurnit (Josh and Howard later went on to found First Round Capital, generally considered the country's leading early stage venture capital fund). Members either invest individually or, more typically, pool their investments with other New York Angels and serve as lead investor for that investment. Each member makes his or her own thorough review of all information, including speaking with representatives of the company. In late 2012, the New York Angels created an entrepreneur catalyst fund to support the funding needs of even earlier stage start-ups.

The New York Angels has to date invested over $50 million in more than 70 early stage businesses. The group, made up of CEOs, entrepreneurs, VCs, and business leaders who have led successful organizations, is known for a commitment to mentoring and coaching the entrepreneurs in whom it invests. Members often serve on founders' boards, provide contacts, and assist with team building, strategic planning, and future fundraising. The group typically manages opportunities from $100,000 to $1 million. For investments above $2 million, the New York Angels syndicates with other angel groups. New York Angels was the first member of the Angel Capital Association, the professional trade group of American angel investor organizations.

A number of angel groups pool their money in advance into a single fund and as a result function much like seed-level VCs that vote as a group on an investment. Some of them focus on specific interests. Golden Seeds is an angel network with an affiliated venture fund that is dedicated to the empowerment of women entrepreneurs and the people who invest in them. Golden Seeds typically invests in startups where a female corporate-level executive owns a significant amount of the business.

The Golden Seeds angel network, consisting of 250 investors (both men and women), is the fourth largest in the United States and was the third most active in 2011. Its venture capital group of eight managing partners currently has two funds with $30 million under management and investments in 26 portfolio companies. The firm also provides training in angel and venture investing through an academy consisting of over 30 educational modules. Started in 2004 by Stephanie Newby (also a New York Angels member), Golden Seeds has headquarters in New York, offices in Boston and San Francisco, and investor affiliates in Los Angeles and Dallas.

ANGELS AND VCs

The major difference between angel investors and venture capitalists (VCs) is the source of the funds and, generally, the amount of money they invest.

Angels invest their own money. VCs invest money raised from other investors. There are lots of other differences, but that's the biggest one.

All angels in the United States are high-wealth individuals who are designated "accredited investors." In order to qualify as an angel investor, you must have at least $1 million in assets (not including the value of your home), or income exceeding $200,000 in each of the two most recent years, or joint income with a spouse exceeding $300,000 for those years and a reasonable expectation of the same income level in the current year.

Many novice entrepreneurs make the mistake of thinking of angels and VCs interchangeably. But angels and VCs are two very distinct groups with different goals, attributes, and processes. One way to differentiate between them is to consider the continuum of investment size. David S. Rose, the Founder of New York Angels and my predecessor as its Chairman (and even farther back, a client of mine when I was running TSI), is a prolific contributor to the question and answer website Quora, where he has so far answered over 1,300 questions about startups and angel investing. While there are no hard and fast rules about which investors invest which amounts, David has written the following answer breaking down the startup funding sequence for founders into very rough ranges, as follows:

- **From $0 to $25,000** you will likely be investing your own cash out of your own pocket, otherwise no one else will be comfortable investing at all. Once in, this money stays in, and is part of what makes up your Founder's Equity (along with your work and your intellectual property).

- **From $25,000 to $150,000** you will likely be rounding up friends and family to put in the first outside cash on top of yours. This will usually be documented as either a straight sale of Common Stock (which is most typical) or else as Convertible Note, which converts into the same security as the next professional round, but at a discount (which is actually better for everyone).

- **From $150,000 to $1.5m,** you are in angel territory, either by lucking into one really rich and generous angel, or (more likely) by pulling together either a bunch of individuals (at $10,000–$100,000 each), or one or more organized angel groups, or one or more micro-VCs ("super angels"). Depending on the circumstances, they will invest either in the form of a Convertible Note (but with a cap on valuation), or else in a Series Seed or Series A Convertible Preferred stock round, using similar documentation to that used by VCs.

- **From +/– $1.5m up to, say, $10m,** you're looking at early stage venture capital funds, which will almost certainly be using something very much like the National Venture Capital Association's Model Series A documents. They will likely make their first investment about half of what they're prepared to put in, with the rest coming in one or more follow-on rounds if you execute successfully on your plan.

- **Finally, north of, say, $10m to $20m,** you'd be getting money from a later stage venture capital fund, whose paperwork will be similar to the earlier VCs. They will put in much larger amounts of cash, but your valuation will be much, much higher, so they may end up with a smaller stake than the earlier investors (who would likely have continued to invest in each round in order to maintain their percentage ownership.)

Although this is the canonical progression, keep in mind that the number of companies that get all the way through it is very, very, VERY small. A majority of companies that are started in the U.S. begin and end with the first stage: the founders' own money. The number of companies that are able to get outside funding then begins to drop by orders of magnitude: the percentages (again, very, rough) are that 25 percent of startups will get Friends & Family money; 2.5 percent will get angel money; 0.25 percent will get early stage VC money; and probably 0.025 percent will make it to later stage VCs.

RISKS OF LETTING VCs INTO YOUR SEED ROUND

Some angels say it's not a good idea to mix angels and VCs in the seed round. "It doesn't matter if the big VC invests under a different name or merely provides space and mentoring," says early stage investor and serial entrepreneur Chris Dixon. "If a big VC has any involvement with your company at the seed stage, their posture toward the next round has such strong power that they can kill you and/or control the pricing of the round."

The decision to accept equity from VCs in the seed round extends the time to exit by a decade or more, according to Basil Peters, author of *Early Exits: Exit Strategies for Entrepreneurs and Angel Investors (But Maybe Not Venture Capitalists)*. He acknowledges that the exit data he has amassed is not yet conclusive, but the implications are clear:

> If a company accepts financing from venture capital investors, the minimum exit valuation per share has to be 10–30 times more than the price the VCs paid. Holding out for a very high value exit will dramatically reduce the chances of success and statistically extend the exit time for the angels and entrepreneurs by over a decade.

The venture capital investors will almost certainly block any attempt to sell a successful company that does not meet their minimum required returns.

Signaling Effect

The term "signaling effect" is used to describe the problem of VCs making seed investments in startups. The difficulty is that most angels perceive VCs to have access to better information than they themselves do. Angels watch very closely what VCs do. So when a VC makes a seed investment, that's a signal for angels to jump on board if they are offered the opportunity.

So far, so good. But the signaling effect becomes a problem when a VC makes a seed investment in a startup but then for whatever reason doesn't follow through with an investment in the next round. Everyone then assumes the VC knows something damaging about the startup and backs off. In other words, investors assume that by declining to make a subsequent investment in the startup, the VC is "sending a signal" that something is wrong with the company. The signaling effect kills the round. The higher the profile of the VC, the more profound the signaling effect.

I accept that there are risks to mixing angels and VCs, but sometimes the benefits outweigh the risks. I ask startups to consider three such benefits:

1. Angels often find great investments that they would like to "tee up" for selected VCs to support, facilitating the all-important follow-on round.

2. Some VCs prefer to invest in startups that have smart, industry-knowledgeable angels behind them.

3. The VC round is a seed-level round, and they want other seed-level money.

I've met hundreds of angels in my career, and I can tell you that they all bring different perspectives, strengths, motives, and values to the relationship. If there's one commonality, it's that they are interested in the relationship. Most angels authentically want to have a successful relationship with founders; angels want the founders they invest in to succeed, and not necessarily because they are thinking only of the bottom line.

CHAPTER 2 TAKEAWAYS

- Angel investors invest their own money.

- Few angels are in it only for the money.

- Angel investors realize returns only when a startup exits.

- Accepting seed money from traditional VCs may complicate angel funding.

Let's Get to Know Each Other

3

I am amazed how many emails and calls I get from entrepreneurs who want me to invest in their startups but have not made any effort to find out the most basic information about me. This is an excellent opportunity for them to impress me with their resourcefulness and selling ability. Let me be blunt here. If founders haven't done this basic homework before calling me, I have to believe they will be just as lazy when it comes to calling prospects or customers.

If you want me to invest, it really improves your chances if you do your homework and arrange to get an introduction to me by someone I respect. The ideal way to get my attention is to approach me at an investing symposium, business plan competition, or other speaking venue where I have my investing hat on. Stalking me while I'm with my family at an event unrelated to investing is probably not going to score points for you. Though I have to admit, I was impressed when a cyclist recognized me while I was on my bicycle and pitched me as we rode together on the bike path by the West Side Highway.

You don't have to be Sherlock Holmes here. I'm not exactly the Invisible Man. The startup grid was actually invented for me. Like most active angel investors, I tend to be ego-driven, welcome visibility, and encourage anyone with a serious startup to reach out to me. I've tried to be as open and transparent about my business, investing, and philanthropic activities as possible. I think the same is true for a majority of the active angel investors I know. We're out there. Many angels have personal websites, maintain blogs, and are active tweeters. Others have written books, been visible on cable TV shows, or have posted videos on YouTube and other sites.

Entrepreneurs often thank me for my time. I always remind them that it's not necessary to thank me. I couldn't be an angel investor if it wasn't for them.

By now I'm a relatively well-known quantity in angel investing circles. I lecture on angel investing and entrepreneurship at forums around the country. I've coached or judged dozens of university business plan competitions. For better or for worse, my reputation as an angel is established for those who have the desire to explore. The plain fact of the matter is that it's not difficult for founders to know basic facts about me or any other serious angel investor before they pick up the phone. In many ways each of us wants to be recognized for our individual business accomplishments, investment prowess, and mentorship.

KNOW THE OUTCOME

What do you want? Not generally, not a year from now, but what, specifically, do you want to happen as a result of meeting with me? It's critical that you get this part right. I'm not going to fund your startup based on our initial meeting, so if that's your outcome, you're going to be disappointed. In fact, the only reasonable outcome of our first meeting is for me to agree to a second meeting or to recommend you to the New York Angels for screening.

Another outcome is for me to give you my business card and say "contact me."

Adapt your pitch to the context. The goal of each pitch, for me, is to allow me to offer advice. My job is to do everything possible to help you better prepare for funding even if I'm not the person who's ultimately going to invest. All too often, startups put too much information in the early pitches.

Another outcome you may want is for me to say, "That's interesting. Tell me more." I am interested in the "why" of the business, not just an explanation of an idea. In a sea of pitch noise, the ones that stand out are usually the simplest in concept and easiest for me to appreciate in terms of the customer value proposition.

To achieve this, you should have a very well-practiced elevator pitch that will intrigue me. Be prepared to give me a concise summary of your business. The trick is to give me just enough that I want to know and understand more. Generate curiosity. Most startups go overboard and give me the whole load, leaving me confused and overburdened to find the real story of their business. Less really is more.

THE PERFECT ELEVATOR PITCH

The first thing I generally want to hear is your elevator pitch: a short, well-crafted explanation of the problem you solve, how you solve it, and how big a market there is for that solution. At the end of the chapter, I offer specific tips for perfecting your elevator pitch.

Remember, your elevator pitch isn't a sales pitch. You don't need to "sell" me on anything, nor should you design it to "close" me. Your opportunity should speak for itself. That said, there's every reason for you to position the opportunity in a memorable way. There's an art and science to perfecting the elevator pitch. If you're struggling to come up with a memorable elevator pitch, here are some suggestions.

Consider the most fundamental problems your product or service solves. Then create a short one-sentence statement for each. Don't sweat the wording just now. Just talk them out as if you were talking to your best friend.

Mark Levy, the founder of Levy Innovation, makes his living helping people brand themselves. His clients hire him to help craft their elevator pitches. Elevator pitches inspired by Mark's counsel are known for a distinctive phrasing that begins "You know how when . . ." The idea is to complete that thought by identifying the problem the product or service addresses and then suggesting one memorable detail about how to make the need real as opposed to a pie-in-the-sky possibility. For example, the elevator pitch for the developer of the first TV remote control might have said, "You know how when you're watching TV from your easy chair, you need to get up to change the channel or the volume? Well, my product allows you to control the TV from the comfort of your chair just by pushing a button."

FIVE TIPS FOR PERFECTING YOUR ELEVATOR PITCH

The point of an "elevator pitch" is to get the angel interested enough in your startup to give you a business card or refer you to someone else who might be interested. You don't need to reel them in; you just need to get them on the hook. Here are five ways to make sure your pitch gets an investor. In the end, it's really about the investor being able to repeat the story accurately to other angels and get them excited.

1. **Less is more.** Angels appreciate conciseness. Make it clear, make it sing, but most of all, make it short. The duration must be less than the typical elevator ride. Make that the express elevator. No more than 30 seconds or about 150 words,

max. Don't guess on this. Have someone time you, and then practice your delivery so you can do it from memory.

2. **Problem-solution.** Explain the problem or challenge that a customer would be willing to pay to solve, and describe at least one way your product solves that problem.

3. **More concrete than abstract.** Many elevator pitches stay on the surface, espousing "big ideas" through generalization and abstraction. Concrete details make a dent in the angel's mind.

4. **Be specific.** Avoid general "business speak," or your elevator pitch will sound like one that dozens of startups could use. The telling image captures the attention of angels and coaxes us into action and repeating. Make it specific to your product or service.

5. **Practice, practice, practice.** And then practice some more.

MORE CHUTZPAH, PLEASE

If you're uncomfortable about delivering a sharp-as-a-tack elevator pitch, then you're not ready to run your startup. If you are not ready to approach an approachable guy like me, how on earth are you going to get meetings with the customers, suppliers, and partners that are essential to your business success? If you can't muster the assertiveness to get through an angel investor's relatively open door, how are you going to persuade impatient prospects to give you the time of day, or journalists to cover your launch, or high-performing employees to join your fledgling startup?

In other words, I expect great founders to have more than their share of chutzpah. Patrick Ambron, CEO of BrandYourself.com, is a great example of what I mean. Using

LinkedIn, AngelList, and TechCrunch (I'll discuss each of these tools in Chapter 10), Ambron made a careful list of the angels he thought would be most receptive to investing in BrandYourself. By dutifully leveraging relationships, he got an audience with every one of the angels he targeted. That every angel immediately turned him down didn't intimidate him. Ambron promised to keep in touch, he followed through, and as I'll describe in Chapter 5, he converted every single one into an investor. That's what I call chutzpah.

I'm particularly interested in BrandYourself because, as I mentioned in my introduction, my son Trace cofounded the startup with his college roommate while they were undergraduates at Syracuse University. BrandYourself is a do-it-yourself, personal search engine optimization (SEO) platform that makes it easy for anyone to take control of their own Google results. They provide a free feature that informs you when you are Googled by a specific company and where it is located. Launched in March 2012, BrandYourself has a freemium business model. A free version allows users to monitor up to three personal websites or LinkedIn profiles. For extended features, you can sign up for a premium subscription service.

If you were going to target angels for a business like BrandYourself, what would you look for? Obviously, Ambron looked for angels who invested in startups similar to BrandYourself. He identified a number of angels who invested in search. One of the first angels he contacted was Barney Pell, who was at the time head search strategist at Microsoft and architect and development manager at Bing. Ultimately, Pell became an investor and mentor. Ambron also sought out angels who invested in consumer-facing startups that make formerly complicated things simple. Angels that invested in startups like Klout and Mint.com eventually came on board. "The moral of the story," Ambron says, "is if you're going to solicit from an angel, you have to know them and what they invest in."

The story of how Ambron transformed angels who first said "no" into angels who wrote checks is instructive. Remember, he carefully selected a shortlist of angels, succeeded in using his connections to get an opportunity to meet, and every single angel turned him down. Ambron took it all in stride. Over the next several months, he kept in email contact with the angels, sending short, chatty announcements about his progress. Every once in a while, he would send an email saying, "This week, we accomplished A and B, but we're having trouble with C. Do you have any suggestions?"

To most angels, an email phrased like that is irresistible. Most angels like to help when we can do so in a limited and focused way. All the angels who originally said no responded. Ambron thanked them profusely for the feedback and continued to send updates and the occasional question. The angels must have liked what they saw. By the time BrandYourself was ready for Series A financing, every one of the angels Ambron initially targeted were so familiar with his business and him that they came in.

While Trace was actively the founder in the startup during his Syracuse University days, the team asked me for advice and funding at various points in its evolution. The advice I was pleased to offer, but I held back from investing. The team was winning business plan competitions left and right, yet I didn't see a scalable business model there. Eventually Trace graduated, sold most of his stake in the company, and now we put our energy into a new startup called Launch.it. I'm glad that BrandYourself has assembled such a respected team of angels, and I wish them luck.

BASIC QUESTIONS

Here's the basic information I expect startups to know about me before they contact me. (Later in this chapter I'll talk about *how* I'd like to be contacted.) A decent LinkedIn search or a few phone calls will give interested parties all the information they need to know:

- Who is Brian Cohen?

- What's his background?

- Why does he invest?

- What is he primarily looking for?

- What has he invested in?

- What added value does he provide?

Basically, I'd like to see evidence that the founder *is* an interested party. I want to be convinced that the founder has determined there's the likelihood, based on his or her research about my interests and investing record, that I will be particularly intrigued by the ideas behind the benefits and value the company provides its customers.

Do your research and make the pitch personal to me. That's right, personal. The personal is what—at first—I relate to. You've heard of high-touch products—products designed to appeal first to the senses and then secondarily to the intellect. High touch products—think the iPad, perfume, Champagne—do not come with instruction manuals. Make me feel something for you and the business you plan to create.

EIGHT QUESTIONS I ASK FOUNDERS

Why are you doing a startup? This is your opportunity to tell me about your personal commitment to the business. Is it a burning need you've had for years, or a response to a college business plan competition? Did it flow from your time in a business when you saw an unmet business need? Or is it in the end about your desire for wealth and independence? To get a sense of who you are, I tend to ask these eight questions, when applicable.

1. **What is your burn rate?** This is an investor term referring to how fast money is being spent. The implicit question is how long the startup can survive before breakeven or another cash infusion is required. Unless you have received money to develop your initial product, you should raise money for at least a 12- to 18-month runway.

2. **How much "skin" is already in the game?** The intent of this question is to determine the level of commitment—in both cash and "sweat equity"—of founders, and how much others have already invested into the startup.

3. **How did you get here?** Every startup starts with an early journey that defines how it has reached its current state. Are there founders no longer involved who still own stock? Gaps in the history of a startup are big red flags, just like gaps in your résumé.

4. **How well do the founders get along with each other?** The smartest people are often the most eccentric, so some conflict in the ranks is normal. Excessive conflict, lack of communication, or lack of mutual respect is indicative of a dysfunctional team and eventual failure of the startup.

5. **Who's on your advisory board?** I'd like to know who's advising you and what connections they have.

6. **Can I talk to a real customer?** Real customers are ones who have paid full price for the product, installed it, and are satisfied. Free trials don't count, betas don't count, and "excited about the potential" doesn't count. If there are no customers yet, when will the product ship?

7. **How solid is the intellectual property?** Provisional patents or lawsuits pending don't add up to a strong sustainable competitive advantage.

8. **Are you incorporated in the United States?** I'm glad to invest in entrepreneurs from wherever they originate or choose to live. But the startup must be incorporated in the United States.

HOW DO I WANT TO BE CONTACTED?

Every angel investor is different. In this section, I've asked a number of angel investors to describe how they wish to be contacted. But speaking for myself, there's a simple thing I want a founder to do before he or she calls or, better yet, sends me an email.

I'd like the founder to attend a presentation where I am speaking. I generally participate in an average of three such meetings every week. I want you to come and listen to me for two reasons. First, if you make that investment to check me out, I will be glad to give you the same courtesy. Second, show up and see if we personally connect.

Meetings are a great way to make initial contact. At that point, I'm in my most intense social mood, and the settings for my radar for new opportunities are at the maximum. I make myself available and accessible at such meetings. If my schedule allows, I will stick around until everyone who wants to meet with me gets a chance. That's really why I'm there.

When I speak at such meetings, it's not because I want to hear myself talk. Rather, I want to hear from people like you who have something novel to share and can teach me something new. Come talk to me. Have a comment or two about some point that I've made. Add your perspective. Show me that you've learned something. Challenge me, if you have the facts to back it up.

Opening this personal door to the earliest moments of idea sharing is what makes angel investing most stimulating.

Here are a few things you can do to get me to sit up and take notice. The most disarming approach is to reference something we have in common. That is usually easier than it might appear. Did you know I went to Syracuse University as an undergraduate? That I attended Boston University for my masters, and for many years I was passionately involved in the school? That I am formally or informally associated with a half dozen other universities? That I'm launching my own startup?

Did you know I got my start as the publisher of a computer magazine? That with my wife, Carol, I cofounded one of the largest high-tech public relations companies in the United States? Can you find a point of entry into any of these chapters of my life? If you can, I'll want to sit down with you. Prepare to talk about what it is that we have in common for a while before we get to your opportunity. I know you want to get to what you're most passionate about, but trust me, your patience will be rewarded if you start with what *I'm* passionate about.

Claim any kinship to me and I'll be immediately interested, not only because of the kinship but because you've demonstrated you have made an effort to know me. Do we have friends in common? Did you see me on a panel, and did you ask that smart question? Have you read something I've written? These are just some of the most obvious things that you can cite to establish an early connection.

Angel investing is a personal activity that is nourished by personal connections. Have I invested (hopefully with some success) in your industry? Or have I at least failed with some tangible takeaway that has made me smarter? Have I ever built a business myself that might actually be relevant to the business you're in? Do I fit a certain characteristic associated with your industry? Let me know that there's something in my background, some knowledge I control that you think would be advantageous to the success of your business. I really want to be connected to you and your company in some important way other than writing a check. If I give you money, I really want to invest on the basis of your demonstrated appreciation of my skills or background.

I'm a curious guy. I don't know a single active angel investor who isn't. Whet my curiosity. Try to intrigue me even if we didn't go to the same school or don't have anything obvious in common. Take a chance. Mention a hobby of yours or a recent international travel experience or a fun fact about yourself or anything you think might interest me. If you begin by doing some homework and making those linkages or, failing that, taking a flight of imagination, you're going to find yourself on a much more effective path. Even if I don't invest in you, the path will be more pleasant for both of us. In short, make it fun.

Esther Dyson, an old friend and fellow New York Angel, is one of the smartest and most prolific angel investors in the world. At a recent conference of angel investors, I heard her tell the crowd why she's an angel: because she's having fun doing so. I don't think there was an angel in the room who disagreed with her.

There are few angels as visionary and influential as Esther Dyson. She's been an early investor in some of the most successful tech startups, including Google, TrustedID, Cygnus Solutions, Flickr, del.icio.us, Eventful, Netbeans, Powerset, ZEDO, CV-Online, Medscape, Medstory, and Meetup. Since 2007, she has focused on startups in the private aviation and commercial space sector. She's invested in XCOR, Constellation Services, Zero-G, Icon Aircraft, and Space Adventures. Esther's passion is boundless. She has completed cosmonaut training in Russia and is waiting for an opening to travel to space.

I asked Esther what she looks for in prerevenue startups. The common denominator is that she's personally excited about the early idea or the personalities of the founders. Her description of how much she enjoys spending time with her startups is infectious. She invests, first, for personal satisfaction; monetary returns then flow as a consequence of choosing wisely and mentoring well. The mentor commitment is something Esther believes angels should take more seriously. "Most angels sincerely intend to be advisors to their startups and start out that way, but due to time constraints, many angels gradually lose touch," she says. This is understandable, she adds, but regrettable, because it not only reduces the personal satisfaction the angel gets from investing, but the investment suffers as well.

Esther Dyson's view of angel investing is exactly my own. I love the kick I get from it. I love meeting bright young people, listening and learning about all their ideas, and helping them succeed so they, in turn, can inspire and fund other young people. I get a tremendous sense of satisfaction from thinking about the big picture.

THE SINGLE BEST QUESTION TO ASK ME

Founders ask me all kinds of questions, from savvy to silly. But you want to know the best question I have ever been asked by a founder? Here it is: "What excites you about my business?"

That's a question that really gives me a kick. It totally connects with me as a high-touch investor who invests by the thrill I get down my spine. (I've always called this my Spidey Sense, which, as I describe in Chapter 4, was instrumental in me funding a startup called comiXology.) When I see smart entrepreneurs deeply thinking about what they're doing in a captivating way, it's easy for me to share their excitement. Yes, a question like this puts me on the spot, but I welcome being put on the spot.

So the question gets my juices flowing because now I really have to articulate what it is that I really think, what possibilities I envision, what opportunities I can help create by investing. It brings me into your world and forces me to understand what you're trying to do. All of a sudden, I'm speaking on your behalf.

It's so much more than "Please, give me a check." It's "I appreciate what you, Brian, can bring to my startup, and I don't want to waste your time if there is not a good match here."

PUBLICSTUFF

Let me tell you about a startup founder who approached me just the right way. Lily Liu is the founder and CEO of PublicStuff, a New York–based social enterprise that aims to increase civic participation in communities across the nation by helping municipalities, universities, and other institutions receive service requests from their residents or customers in real time. You see a pothole you think the city should fix? There's now an app for that.

PublicStuff helps get broken stuff fixed.

The PublicStuff app makes every resident an extension of the town's repair crew. They see something that needs fixing, they take a photo, and the dispatcher at the town public works department receives the alert and dispatches a crew to address the issue. The app captures the exact location so the resident doesn't need to do more than take a photo. No need to wait for office hours, either. The app works 24/7.

Oh, and the resident gets an email indicating that the issue has been logged and another when the GPS issue is fixed. Residents can also browse lists of existing requests on the website and see a map of the town with maintenance request sites flagged in green. I knew that NYC has been spending huge sums of money trying to figure out the best way to solve this problem. Enter the amazing Lily Liu.

I loved the concept as soon as I heard Liu describe it. PublicStuff helps make municipal governments accountable and transparent, keeping residents in the loop as they go about the business of keeping communities orderly and safe.

I first met Liu as she was leaving her government job to pursue her dream as an entrepreneur and solve this problem shared by every municipality in the world. I was still relatively new at the angel investing game, but I knew someone who ran a small incubator in New York. I doubt that's what they were called back then, but an incubator is essentially what it was, and I thought it would be of use to Liu. A hallmark of the NYC startup environment is that it is incredibly supportive and always seeks to help entrepreneurs in any way they can.

The next time Liu and I met, I was giving a presentation at Entrepreneurs Roundtable Accelerator, created by my friend Murat Aktihanoglu, from whom we will hear more in Chapter 11. My job was to talk about strategic communications. With my partner and wife, Carol, I had run a strategic PR business for many years, so I talked about media relations, news releases, newsletters, and other aspects of a coordinated public relations strategy. There were about 25 young entrepreneurs in the room. One of the last things I said was, "Is there anyone here who needs my help to write a news release?" Liu's hand alone went up. So I worked with Lily on the news release, and I was impressed with how PublicStuff had evolved. At that point, she still wasn't quite ready for angel investment, but I knew she soon would be.

When it came time for Liu to raise early-stage capital for PublicStuff, she went to a number of sources, met with a lot of success, and then came to the New York Angels to complete her first round of financing. Her story was so incredible that 18 angels wanted to invest in PublicStuff. Now, that doesn't happen all that often, but that kind of demand creates problems for any founder fortunate enough to face that situation. How was she to decide on which angels to tap? Without my prompting, she asked the question that I urge all founders—and not just the ones in Liu's enviable position—to ask: "Why should I take your money?"

Some of the 18 investors were taken aback. "I'm sorry," one angel said. "You're asking me why you should take my money over somebody else's?" I loved the question, and she must have appreciated my response because I ended up investing in PublicStuff, which is to say I ended up investing in Lily Liu.

For other angels, it wasn't a comfortable moment, but Liu, to her credit, held her ground and listened. She ended up taking money from three other angel investors, the ones that Liu felt brought the most commitment and relevant experience to her startup. You might say the founder of PublicStuff accessed "smart money," but whatever you call it, her choices were born from a sense of confidence and a very clear understanding of the needs of her juggernaut business. To me, Lily Liu represents a new and very positive trend among entrepreneurs in a world of plentiful angel money.

FEAST WITH ME

So, you want me to invest in your startup? I think of the most attractive investment opportunities as sumptuous buffets. Startups are my business, and I couldn't do it without you. So let's talk and feast.

I've learned that there's nothing more important than breaking bread with you, ideally over a number of meals. I rarely invest in a business without having at least one enjoyable meal with the founder. Smart angel investing requires we develop a partnership of mutual opportunity. I want to dine on your ideas and dreams.

There is just something about dining with someone. It's different than a transactional, agenda-driven presentation/business meeting. Dining is more casual and relaxed. It's simply a better way to get connected to people. A meal is familiar. I can tell a lot about people by how they relate to food.

I regard a startup investment opportunity as being akin to setting a fabulous buffet. Like a well-planned series of meals, I want to have everything in order. I want to be guided through the full progression of a meal, and I want a whole day's nourishment going from breakfast and lunch to dinner. If you want me to be an angel investor-partner, please join me for the feast. I guarantee that in the end, we will both feel satisfied.

Breakfast

Breakfast is my favorite meal of the day. It's the meal where all things are possible. Launching a business is akin to greeting the morning. It requires opening fresh eyes to something refreshing, something quite possibly never seen before. I want to begin the morning with you, to see the sunrise, to enjoy the smell of pancakes on the griddle.

So please join me for breakfast to welcome new beginnings. We are not going to dwell on your business. I just want to know a little more about you. Have you squeezed an orange for my juice, or did you open a can of concentrate? Is that Canadian bacon I smell, or burnt toast? I want to be intrigued about the omelet you order. I want to finish breakfast wanting to know and enjoy more.

Lunch

If I invite you to lunch, you know I'm intrigued and want to continue the conversation. Now I'm looking for more detail about your idea. I want to find out more about what makes you tick and your deeper insights for the business. Don't be shy about asking me anything. I want to appreciate that you understand that we are connecting, that a beneficial relationship is being born. Because it's only over lunch that I can really appreciate who you are and the team supporting you and the concepts associated with the business.

By the end of lunch, I can end up feeling overfed with too much information. So maybe you'll offer me an espresso—some specific jolting input that will help me get back on track. Better yet, you'll suggest a follow-up for when I'm ready to connect all the dots. If you're savvy, you'll come back to me after lunch to keep me informed and excited about the opportunity. Then, if I'm still with you, I will invite you to dinner. That's the big show.

Dinner

Dinner is where I'm really determined to get inside your head to learn about you and your business through careful *due* and *do* diligence. (See Chapter 10 for more about what I mean by *due* and *do* diligence.) I'm going to ask you about the issues that make a difference, about your business plan, and about the marketplace you are entering. I'm going to want to talk to your customers to see how far you've come. I want to understand the depth of your technical perspective and the maturity of your business approach.

I'll ask you to describe the launch you envision for your product or service. Only then can we get into the issues. That's where I come in as a resource. I see myself as an ongoing mentor to those who at this point have earned my respect and allegiance. I need to know beyond a shadow of a doubt that you want me as a partner and appreciate in a concrete way the specific leverage I can offer you.

So let's turn to our dinner. I'm fascinated about what you order. The best entrepreneurs don't limit themselves to items they have already tasted. They want to try something original, experience a new taste sensation. That goes for investors, too. Smart investors are never satisfied with the same meal. And let's not forget the side dishes, the additions to the meal that bring outside credibility. This is where incubators and accelerators can fit in to solidify an idea or to build partnerships.

You can certainly select from the menu, but can I interest you in a few of the investor specials? The right angel investor can offer an incredibly nutritious stream of experience, launch insights, and contacts. If you are closed to this avenue of input, you are losing out on a wealth of wisdom from an experienced palate. Angel investors will help set the table for your offering in ways you may not have considered. Technically and financially, they can help you create relationships that will advance your opportunity. Prepare to be satiated by all the resources available to you. It's you who will be feasting.

The Check, Please

An investing opportunity, like a meal, involves more than just empty calories. It has to be nutritious for everyone. Yes, the money is critical, but it's really about creating relationships, an ambience that persists long after the meal is complete. The opportunity is about whom we invite to the table and how open we are with each other when we sit down. Angel investors, like great hosts, know that the company is as important as the meal itself and that long after the soup is forgotten, the relationships forged over a series of meals create enduring opportunities for mutual profit.

HIGH-TOUCH INVESTOR

I'm an unrepentant high-touch investor. I'm initially energized by emotional motives and appeals to the senses. I definitely do not want to start with the instruction manual (e.g., PowerPoint presentation). I'm speaking for myself here, but I think many angel investors react much the same way. We see thousands of proposals, all making unlikely representations.

I'm energized by people, social settings, good meals, freewheeling conversations. What I focus on first is the entrepreneur's judgment, character, resilience, and sense of humor. Yes, investing ends up as a series of formal business transactions, but for me at least, it begins as a personal partnership.

Remember, I'm investing my own money. When I fund a startup, I write a check from my personal checking account. That's a huge difference between most angels and VCs. With the possible exception of sharing a toothbrush, there's nothing more personal than giving someone a substantial sum of money. (I'm aware that some angel funds are pooled from many investors, including me occasionally, but for now I'm talking about those cases where I am the individual investor.) The bottom line for me: it's personal. I want founders to really appreciate that they are embarking on a special and personal relationship with me. The money issues come later.

Of course, angel investing is not quite as much fun when I'm losing money. Ultimately, I need to get a positive financial return out of the relationship. People considering angel investments will often call me and ask, "How are you doing?" by which they mean "Are you making a profit?" At some point, all angels need to be able to answer that question in the affirmative. Eventually, I need to see a return on my investments. Otherwise, I'm not conducting a business but a hobby, and do you really want a hobbyist as a business partner?

CHAPTER 3 TAKEAWAYS

- The only thing you have is time; don't waste it.

- Do your research and make the pitch personal to me.

- Never waste an introduction or an opportunity to meet somebody who can help you.

- The only reasonable outcome from a first meeting with me is a second meeting with me.

What I'm Looking for in an Entrepreneur

What am I looking for in an entrepreneur? I can answer that question in one word.

You.

You, the entrepreneur, are the single most important element of a potential investment. The entire purpose of your pitch is to convince me that you are the special entrepreneur in whom I feel comfortable investing my money and time.

Let's face it. Someone is going to have to run your business every day, and it's not going to be me. It all comes down to you.

So be true to yourself. If you take away just one piece of advice from this chapter, let it be this: understand your absolute responsibility, and be the person who makes it all happen. The rabbis of old tell the story of the great Rabbi Zusha, who was on his deathbed, surrounded by his family, friends, and students. They saw him crying and asked if he was in distress because he feared death. "It's not death that I fear," Rabbi Zusha explained, "but that when I meet my Maker, I will be asked a question that will prove my lack of merit."

One of the students asked, "Is the question you fear, 'Why were you not more like Moses?'"

The rabbi shook his head no. "The question I fear is 'Why were you not more like Zusha?'"

It's tempting to try to be the person you imagine investors want you to be. Please don't succumb. Even if you could get away with it, you'll have gained nothing. After seeing more than a thousand presentations, I can spot a con job a thousand yards away. It's critical that we both respect reality.

You will exhaust yourself trying to make sense of what everyone expects in a dynamic startup. Being true to yourself is what leadership requires—to look at the chaos and provide an honest point of view about needs to be met first, second, and third. People want to work with leaders who are comfortable with themselves while setting the point of view with clarity and conviction.

START THE PRESENTATION WITH YOU

So remember, you are the first and most important element of the presentation. The focus of the presentation should start and conclude with you. The biggest mistake entrepreneurs make in their pitches is to allow the focus to shift from them to the graphs and pretty images on their PowerPoint presentations.

In Chapter 5, I offer a number of insightful tips on how to tailor your pitch to keep the focus where it belongs. But for now, let me ask you a quick question: Who is the best presenter in recent business history? Does anyone doubt it's the late Steve Jobs? He changed the way presentations are inspired, designed, and delivered. Now, I want you to visualize Steve presenting. The iconic image is that of a slim man in a black turtleneck and New Balance athletic shoes all alone on a bare stage, with a huge blank presentation screen. And what's on the screen when Steve walks in? Initially, nothing. Maybe the iconic Apple logo. Steve wanted all eyes on him and not on the screen. And even when something appeared on the screen, it was rarely more than a headline or a word. Or even better, an image. Apple knew that as important as the announcement of the iPhone or iPad was, the real story was Steve Jobs. Everyone knew Steve was in charge and clearly knew where his company was headed. He became the personification of Apple and its products. You could do worse than aspire to be the personification of your particular brand.

Yes, the business case and financials are important, but they come later. In the 10 or 15 minutes that you have for the pitch, I want you to shine and leave me with no question but that you have three critical characteristics: integrity, determination, and street smarts. If you show me those right away, I'll listen closely and stick around for the rest of the pitch. If you can't signal integrity and entrepreneurial proficiency in the first 45 seconds, you've more than likely lost me. Let me says a few words about these three key characteristics.

INTEGRITY

Integrity comes first for most investors. For me, it's a deal-breaker. If I am not absolutely, positively persuaded that you—and the startup's top management team—have a track record of integrity, I will not invest, even if you could guarantee—which you couldn't—that my investment will absolutely, positively pay off.

As an entrepreneur, you are selling some future good. As an angel, I'm investing in your promise to create and build a business that doesn't yet exist. That promise becomes, as in politics, uniquely tied to your character.

By integrity, I mean more than just general characteristics such as ethics, honesty, and trustworthiness. Those are the minimums, but I expect more.

Authenticity, for example.

Authenticity is the only way you can tell your story to the world in a believable way. Save your spinning for the fitness center. I can see right through it, and so can most potential customers.

PREVIOUS ENTREPRENEURIAL EXPERIENCE

Like most angels, I love to invest in serial entrepreneurs. Just to know that you have participated in taking a business from beginning to end is enormously reassuring. There is simply no substitute for demonstrating that you know what it takes to launch a startup. The ideal outcome is that you can also demonstrate an exit, but that's not as critical as you may think. Even a failed startup is not a deal-breaker. I want to know that you have walked the walk, faced the fears, and sped forward toward a vision.

Everyone has to start somewhere. The important thing is to start.

Don't be too concerned if you lack significant entrepreneurial experience. The reality is that most of the startups I consider aren't led by serial entrepreneurs. Most are led by founders doing their first startups. That's fine. Everyone has to start somewhere. But in such cases, I want to see evidence of starting or running something. It can be a college club or a volunteer activity. Any entrepreneurial activity counts. The point is, you've put yourself out there, organized a team, and provided leadership to a common objective.

LEADERSHIP CHEMISTRY
AND MANAGEMENT EXPERIENCE

Another thing I look for when investing in a startup is leadership and management experience.

Starting a successful business can be a frustrating exercise in team building, where the area of leadership is first tested. Founders will need to make smart hires to form small, powerful teams with good chemistry. They will then have to coordinate the work of those teams, inspire them to execute flawlessly, and develop a product or service that succeeds in disrupting the existing marketplace, usually in a hostile marketplace populated by organizations with much greater financial resources.

That's why I want you to convince me you have leadership and management skills in spades or, lacking that, you can develop them in the near future. Leadership experience that has been tested is the best demonstration you can offer. But I also value other forms of leadership experience. The key for founders is to show that they have previously built a team and successfully executed a complex plan.

DOMAIN KNOWLEDGE

For me, domain knowledge is critical. How can you go into a business and not know it cold? If you tell me you're going to be the great developer in human genome mapping, you'd better know what a human genome is. Domain expertise means more than in-depth knowledge about the technical aspects of a subject. It should embrace the marketplace space in which you plan to compete. Do you breathe your customer's air? Do you feel what your customers feel?

You'd be surprised how often I get pitched by entrepreneurs who have very shallow ideas about the business space they propose to disrupt. They are ignorant about the competitive issues, can't identify the leading competitors in the space, and haven't determined the demographics of the customers.

You really want to impress me with your domain knowledge? Here's how. Take a month or two and actually work in the industry you intend to enter. In 2009, Lee Lin, the cofounder of RentHop, had an idea for eliminating the rental broker, the guy who stands between apartments and renters. In technical terms, this is called disintermediation. At first blush, it seemed like a decent idea. We've seen the efficiencies that ensued when intermediaries such as travel agents were eliminated. Moreover, I've had my share of bad experiences with brokers, so the startup idea was personal. I resent paying 15 percent of the annual rent for what seems like little work. I was inclined to invest in a startup that could automate away the rental broker. But could RentHop do it?

The answer was no. Lin actually worked as a broker in New York City for a couple of months. First he obtained a New York State broker's license, and then he went to work signing up apartment listings and showing apartments to tenants in Corona, a gritty working class area of the city. Lin actually did pretty well. He closed seven deals in one month. He probably could have earned more working as a rental broker than going the startup route, but he wanted to be an entrepreneur. Alas, as to the question of whether rental agents really offered little value and were therefore expendable, the simple answer was no, they could not. By working on the ground floor of the industry, he concluded that rental brokers, far from being commodities that could be automated away, were an integral part of the transaction and added real value. A pivot for RentHop was required.

Looking at the problem through a lens based on real-world experience, Lin and his partners saw that what the industry really needed was better information about desirable brokers and desirable landlords. RentHop's mission became to simplify the apartment-hunting process through technology and tenant-driven recommendations. RentHop's algorithms are calibrated to show only quality apartments from the most responsive landlords and brokers. The company is profitable. "If your goal is to disrupt and put an entire profession out of business, you'd better know that business inside and out," Lin says.

SKILLS

Skills give teeth to knowledge. It's not enough to know a subject cold. You also have to execute a business plan, and that requires real skills. Show me that you have skills required to assemble and develop a team and get a company going. Then there's an endless list of specialized business skills: marketing, sales, management, finance. Relax. There are very few people who have the full set of skills required to lead a company, let alone a fragile startup. So if you don't have some skills, say so. That's where integrity comes in. Don't pretend to know more than you actually do. It's no sin to lack skills in one thing or another. Perhaps you can learn the skills, and maybe it would be better to outsource the tasks requiring such skills anyway.

STREET SMARTS

A founder with street smarts knows what to expect, anticipates events before they happen, and has a well-earned 360-degree view of the world. Sometimes street smarts allow founders to see around corners.

---

10 PRACTICES OF HIGHLY EFFECTIVE ENTREPRENEURS

I've engaged with thousands of entrepreneurs over the years. As I think about the handful who impressed me enough for me to take out my checkbook, the following 10 attributes stand out. The most highly effective entrepreneurs:

1. **Focus outward, not inward.** They are customer-centric in every decision. They live inside the customer's head.

2. **Make decisions.** Lots of decisions. An entrepreneur told me things were not going well. I asked. "How many decisions did you make last week?" She said, "Very few." I asked, "Then how do you expect things to change?"

3. **Are cheerfully in control.** They believe with every fiber of their being that they can make a difference and enjoy the process. Celebrate everything you can.

4. **Want to serve before being served.** It's about generosity and always creating value and service. A true entrepreneur is sensitive to the needs of employees, partners, investors, etc.

5. **Don't waste time.** It's your most precious commodity.

6. **Keep their promises.** On both the personal and organizational levels.

7. **Are great communicators.** There's a hint of vaudeville in their presentations, formal and informal.

8. **Look at the big picture.** The best leaders are not myopic. They're focused on the business, by all means, but they see how their business interacts and connects to multiple possibilities.

9. **Are smart fast.** It's not enough just to be smart. It's not enough to be fast. You need to be smart fast. If you think you're smart, get smarter. If you think you're fast, get faster.

10. **Zero-base their assumptions.** Constantly challenge yourself to question what you knew to be true yesterday.

INTRODUCING COMIXOLOGY

Over the years, I've been blessed to meet a number of entrepreneurs who have what I'm most looking for—integrity, determination, street smarts—in abundance. It's no disrespect to anyone else to single out David Steinberger, CEO of comiXology, to illustrate what I mean.

David had collected comic books as a kid, and the collection was cluttering up his parent's house. They asked David to clear it out. While he was doing that, he got an idea. There was iTunes for music, and Amazon for books, but a central, curated market for comic books was lacking.

At New York University's Stern School of Business, where he was pursuing an MBA, David developed a website aggregating information about digital comics. The team entered a NYU business plan competition and ended up with first place. I met him shortly thereafter and invested.

Why did I invest in what became comiXology? As an old comic book collector myself—I'm proud to own a number of valuable first editions—the very idea intrigued me. Comic people are fanatics but have tended to age out of readership, because unfortunately comic stores look like a cross between a topless bar and a head shop, and most would not visit them to purchase comics. David shows an unrelenting clarity to position his company to meet one goal: bringing digital comics to people everywhere.

In five short years, comiXology has revolutionized the comic book and graphic novel world. David saw comiXology as a platform for e-commerce in digital comics and services for brick and mortar retailers. That would have been interesting enough, but he also designed the platform as a tool for comics retailers. ComiXology is now the largest digital comic distributor of single issue comics available across iPad, Android, and the Web. In 2011, comiXology's Comics application was the highest-grossing application in the Apple iPhone App Store, and together with the branded applications for other comics publishers, accounted for a majority of the five top-grossing iPhone apps. ComiXology was recently selected as a preloaded app on Amazon's Kindle Fire.

What did I see in David? David has a special intellectual charisma that gets people to buy into his ability to get people to work with him. He has this uncanny sense for making people feel comfortable about believing in him. He has a wonderful boyish charm that ameliorates any concerns about his ability to deliver. Somehow, you know he'll figure it out.

TAKE THE AUDITION SERIOUSLY

Let's face it. There's a certain amount of casting involved in pitching to an angel. It's like an audition, and looks do matter.

Linda Holliday is a media, Internet, and marketing serial entrepreneur and a member of the New York Angels. An Internet veteran, Linda is an active mentor-consultant whose interests center on the intersection between old and new media. She coaches founders to think about the pitch as an audition for a starring role in a movie or play. Linda recently met with a woman who spent her career in the corporate world and had an idea for a startup. I'll let Linda tell the story:

> The woman showed up wearing a black dress, stockings, pumps, and pearls. My feedback: you already don't fit the casting mold for an entrepreneur: your experience is in corporate, with its baggage of being large and slow. By your dress you are reinforcing your origins instead of what you want to be. So dress the new role, not the old role. Broadcast that you understand you are auditioning for a part and you take the audition seriously.

STARTUPS LED BY WOMEN DO BETTER

I pay special attention to startups that are founded by women entrepreneurs or have women as senior executives. My experience is that angel-backed startups led by women have definite advantages in the marketplace over startups where only men are in charge. It stands to reason: women consumers make the majority of purchasing decisions in this country. Businesses with significant female leadership in product design and marketing will tend to outperform companies without such talent.

I look for startups with leadership by women because The Nielsen Company estimates that almost all income growth in the United States over the past 15 to 20 years has been generated by women exercising their growing economic influence. Women today are responsible for 83 percent of all consumer purchases and 55 percent of all consumer electronics, according to Maddy Dychtwald, author of *Influence: How Women's Soaring Economic Power Will Transform Our World for the Better.*

A new report that tracks startups and their investors sponsored by Dow Jones VentureSource found that startups have a greater chance of going public, operating profitably, or being sold for more money than they've raised when they have females acting as founders, board members, C-level officers, vice presidents, and/or directors. At successful companies, the median proportion of female executives was 7.1 percent versus 3.1 percent at unsuccessful companies. The study followed 20,194 U.S.-based companies that either received funding or exited between 1997 and 2011. Only 1.3 percent of the companies had a female founder; 6.5 percent had a female CEO; and 20 percent had one or more female C-level executives, most commonly in sales and marketing roles. The *Women at the Wheel* report does not speculate on why female executives improve a company's chance of success.

Women are underrepresented in virtually every aspect of business, including the startup community. This book is not the place to speculate on the sources of that underrepresentation. All I want to suggest is that gender diversity is good for startups because it drives different points of view when decisions have to be made. Women, for instance, are more likely than men to consider feature-sets, market segments, or brand statements designed to appeal to women. Women also tend to be more concerned about the emotional well-being of their team. As an angel who's seen his share of startup teams blow his investment to shreds because of internal squabbles, the stabilizing presence of women confers a competitive advantage. As the father of a daughter just embarking on an entrepreneurial career, I bring more than an academic or financial interest to this important issue.

Stephanie Newby, founder of Golden Seeds, is committed to supporting women's entrepreneurship and has two pieces of advice for women-led startups. First, she says, relationships matter. "Getting funding is really about building relationships with the people who you think might become investors in your company," she says. That means being a quality communicator who maintains a strong and ongoing relationship with investors.

The second piece of advice for entrepreneurs is to know your numbers. Too few women entrepreneurs have rigorous financial backgrounds or feel comfortable talking the language of finance, she says. That's not necessarily a deal-breaker. Founders can hire a good CFO and bring them along to answer questions. "But that doesn't let women off the hook; they should still know the fundamental numbers of their startup and be able to articulate them at a high level—no hemming or hawing," Newby says.

OTHER ATTRIBUTES I LOOK FOR

In addition to integrity and experience, I look for these attributes before I invest:

A Strong Team

If you give me a choice between investing in an "A" team with a "B" idea, and a "B" team with an "A" idea, I'll take the "A" team every day of the week. The quality of the business idea, of course, is important, but it pales in significance to the quality of the team. Team quality is hard to define, but the chemistry is obvious when you see it. It's just fun to be around teams like that. They tend to easily finish each other's sentences and seem to be having more fun than others in spite of their challenges.

Ideally, I want to see a cohesive team of long-standing solidarity. There are two parts to this. First, I tend not to invest in lone wolves, no matter how brilliant the entrepreneur. What really makes me sit up is hearing from a team whose members have known each other for years and whose skill sets obviously complement each other.

Most of the entrepreneurs I talk to are young, often in their mid-twenties, or even younger. They can't claim significant work experience. I laughed at a recent presentation when the 23-year-old entrepreneur, representing his two partners, earnestly claimed, "Between the three of us, we have over 66 years of life experience!" The joke, told with timing so perfect you could set a clock by it, brought the house down and no doubt inspired many angels to take a closer look.

A new startup launched by the son of my coauthor is a perfect example of the strength of long-lasting founder relationships. Dan Kador launched Keen IO, a mobile analytics startup, with two buddies, Ryan Spraetz and Kyle Wild. What impressed me is that these three were high school buddies at the Illinois Math and Science Academy and then went through the engineering program at the University of Illinois together. After graduation, they shared a house in San Francisco while they started their careers, Dan and Ryan at Salesforce and Kyle at Google.

After five years of tossing around ideas for a startup, the team put together a proposal and submitted it to the TechStars accelerator program, which invited them to San Antonio, Texas, for an intense, twelve-week period of mentoring and fine-tuning their business model and presentation.

On April 23, 2012, the TechStars Cloud Computing Demo Day commenced with Keen IO leading the presentations. Based on Ryan Spraetz's tremendous presentation, Keen IO easily secured angel financing (they had to turn investors away!) and launched in early 2012. The company hired three awsome people and is well on its way.

A Strong Customer Acquisition Model

I want to invest in startups that have a clear-headed, evidence-based understanding of how they will systematically scale the business. That means knowing how much it costs to acquire customers. It means having their fingers on the pulse of their channels, the sizes of the market segments, and the strategies for reaching them.

Understanding the Competition

I don't want to hear "We're totally unique, there's no one else doing what we do." I can assure you that whatever you think you'll be providing your customers, they are meeting their needs in another way.

Willingness to Pivot

When I address groups of entrepreneurs at college business plan competitions or other venues, I often talk about their eventual need to pivot. This certainly surprises them, because they usually think their initial idea is perfect. Such conversations lead to blunt reality checks for entrepreneurs who need to reconsider their plans.

It's not easy to pivot or make changes, to abandon cherished business assumptions. I want to see evidence that the entrepreneur is not only willing to pivot when necessary but eager to do so when business conditions make it necessary.

An active New York Angel, Alain Bankier is one of New York City's earliest successful angel investors. He was one of the first board members of the New York New Media Association, out of which the New York Angels emerged. Alain believes that one of the most difficult things for young entrepreneurs to know is when they have to iterate (to make a small adaptive "on-the-ground" pivot—see Chapter 14) because what they are doing is not working and not likely to work. The confidence that makes many entrepreneurs successful can also limit their scope when push comes to shove. He's heard all the reasons why it's not time for a startup to pivot:

- We can persist. It will work!
- What we have is disruptive, and we need to teach our customers.
- This is what contrarians do.
- The world just doesn't see it yet; we need a little more money for marketing.

"But sometimes it doesn't work," Alain says. "You're too early or you're too late; the market isn't there; customers are too expensive to acquire. As an entrepreneur you have to demonstrate flexibility to know when it's time to pivot. Evidence of flexibility is one of the most important factors that I look for in a team." Can they adapt to change?

Ability to Tell Stories

I'm mesmerized by a good story well told. Good entrepreneurs communicate a kind of truth that resonates with customers and other stakeholders. I tend to repeat stories in which I can insert myself into the action. Great stories allow your vision and messages to be quickly understood and repeated. Everyone wants to be able to tell the story of the next great startup. It helps if the story hits you where you live.

I recently met an entrepreneur at a Shake Shack party in New York who told me a story about a smartphone app he was developing to track the number of days the phone owner spends in and out of New York City. People who live outside of New York but spend more than half the year in the city have a real issue. If they spend more than 186 days in New York—and even one minute within the city limits counts as a day—they have to pay city income taxes on all their income. For even moderately wealthy people, those taxes can be tens of thousands of dollars. Auditors for the city are very aggressive. The burden is on the taxpayers to prove that they were outside the city limits on any particular day.

So the story this founder told really grabbed me. I was drawn to the idea that at the end of the year, the GPS-based app would consolidate details such as E-ZPass records and credit card charges to keep track of the number of days I spend out of New York. I can tell you that when I mentioned this app to my friends, they were all immediately interested in meeting the founder. They needed something like this tool. The extent to which a story is retold is a hallmark of a powerful story.

Follow-Through and an "I'll Do-It" Vibe

I really need to see follow-through. Early stage investing is not for the faint of heart, either for the entrepreneur or the angel investor. We're going to be in this together for up to 10 years before your startup has an exit. So I really need to know you're in this for the long haul. I'm going to look for evidence for such commitment. I need you to convey that you intend to give your last breath to this enterprise. I want to be sure that you will have to be dragged away from your promise to make this startup a winner. And I want to be absolutely convinced that the occasional setback won't derail your commitment. There's never been an angel- or a venture-funded company in which bad things didn't happen. I want to know that you're committed to be there to the very end.

Use words that are proactive, and avoid being tentative. I don't like to hear words and phrases such as:

- Maybe

- Hopefully

- We'll see

- I wish

- Who knows?
- If we do it

Instead, talk about your startup as if it's already a reality, and there are just a few inconsequential details (like early-stage funding) to get out of the way.

PASSION AND VISION

I frequently get questions from entrepreneurs about passion and vision, two intangibles that seem to create a lot of confusion.

Passion

By all means, be passionate about building a business, but "enthusiastic," "energetic," or "committed" may better describe what you're up to. If I see founders getting all passionate about background data scrubbing, for example, more power to them, but frankly, it's hard for me to get all worked up. Passion sometimes gets in the way.

But I do need to see enthusiasm. If you're not enthusiastic (passionate, energetic, committed, take your pick) about your startup, why should I be enthusiastic? And yes, one of the markers of enthusiasm is the amount of your own money that you put at risk. Don't ask me to risk my money in your business if you don't risk any of yours.

Vision

Many angels care more about the vision thing than anything else. For me, a vision is the reason your business exists. Every business starts with a belief. You should be able to finish the sentence, "The main belief I have about my startup is I believe . . ." The details of your response will probably make up the thesis statement for the vision you want me to communicate about your startup.

Books have been written on getting and communicating a vision. But for the purposes of the pitch, all I need to understand is why your Big Idea is so important. An undifferentiated notion of how a product might succeed does not qualify as a vision.

A mission is from the brain. A vision is from the heart. If you accomplish your mission, the vision will be achieved. A clearly articulated vision is important; without a vision, a startup is unlikely to be successful in the short or long term. But I'm not impressed by visions with long time lines. The world is too unpredictable for a vision statement with a time horizon of more than two years to be meaningful.

A vision must be concise, plausible, and disruptive to some current product or trend. In other words, it should be clear how the new product or service offered by the company will change the marketplace for the better, and why customers of the product or service will find it valuable.

The best part about a great a vision statement is that it immediately causes people to buy into it. Angels look for founders who can articulate a clear idea of what their startup will mean to its clients or customers and what challenges it will face, and who can identify a strategy crafted to address both considerations.

As I mentioned, my son and I recently started a company called Launch.it. This is the vision for Launch.it: I believe in a world of extraordinary creativity and innovation, where all new products, services, and ideas should be easy to find, discover, and share.

ISSUES THAT ANGELS THINK ABOUT PRIOR TO INVESTING

- **Characteristics of the entrepreneur.** Integrity, passion, startup experience, domain expertise, functional skills, leadership, commitment, vision, pragmatism, flexibility, in control.

- **Characteristics of the venture.** Team, business model, traction, customer acquisition, scalability, defensibility, capital efficiency, churn, time to breakeven, exit strategy.

- **Characteristics of the market.** Size, growth, concentration, geography, demographics, competition, channels, regulatory environment, technological developments, adjacent markets.

- **Characteristics of the deal.** Valuation, size of raise, amount of investment, form of investment, liquidation waterfall, option pool, board composition, anti-dilution rights, protective provisions, founder vesting.

Source: David S. Rose, CEO, Gust

IF YOU WANT A GOOD COACH, BE COACHABLE

I started this chapter by talking about the importance of your authentic self showing up in the presentation. That's the first thing angels look for as you enter the room. Let me end by talking about the last thing that angels think about as you leave the room. That's coachability, your perceived ability to be flexible in your thinking, nondefensive, and coachable. Note that the critical word in the last sentence is *perceived*. You may be the most coachable founder in the world, but if angels perceive you to be rigid, defensive, or arrogant, you won't be funded. Perception trumps reality.

We angels are in this business because we understand that young entrepreneurs need coaching, and many of us like being coaches. Most of us received great coaching when we were young entrepreneurs, and we are keen to pay that debt forward. We will gravitate toward funding entrepreneurs who understand their limitations, signal that they welcome coaching, and are willing to engage. That doesn't mean we expect them to mindlessly accept our advice. We welcome pushback. But the last thing we want is coaching relationships with entrepreneurs who have their mind made up, resist challenges, and get defensive. "The first thing angels talk about when an entrepreneur leaves the room after a pitch is focused on his or her coachability," says Linda Holliday:

> I'm not going to invest in you if you don't know how to take advice. That doesn't mean that you have to take all the advice you get. Entrepreneurs need to do 20 things, and you can't possibly be experienced in more than 10 of them, so every founder needs to accept coaching. If you resist feedback, you won't be the best entrepreneur you can be. You may already be executing well, but if you can't open your head honestly to take in what people are saying to you and use some judgment to decide what pieces, if any, are valid, then I can't help you.

I see entrepreneurs get agitated by feedback. That's fatal. If you are agitated or threatened by my feedback, fight back. At least I know you've heard me and are taking my objections seriously.

What are the characteristics of good mentorship? It starts with a good mentor. A good mentor should be in tune with the way you think. He or she should appreciate your perspectives and your innovative thinking. An angel isn't always someone who is an investor. It's certainly helpful if they have walked the path you are trying to walk.

Ideally, they should know what it takes to start a business, raise money, build a team, meet a payroll, and the thousand and one different things that startups need to do. The core benefit of the mentor relationship is depending on someone to tell you what you need to know. The hardest thing for a founder to obtain is experience-based truths. In other words, wisdom.

Wisdom is what you are depending upon a mentor to provide. Making introductions, offering specific advice, and so forth are all good, but they are side benefits. The mentor should have a full picture of your business and be able to say, "Wait! Did you consider this or that alternative?" "What are the unaware assumptions operating here?" Or, "No, that doesn't prove what you think you're proving."

To get the most out of your mentor, you must want it. It's not a pit stop moment. It's an ongoing relationship. And mentors cannot be good mentors unless they are consistently involved in your business. If this seems like a lot of work, it is. I don't believe in à la carte or drive-by mentorship.

CHAPTER 4 TAKEAWAYS

- Accept that it's all about you.

- Be authentic in everything you do.

- You're in control.

- Hire people smarter than you.

- Time is your most precious commodity; learn to invest it in a focused manner on the most important tasks.

What I Look for
in the Pitch

5

If you're invited to the New York Angels, you'll have 15 minutes, some of which might be reserved for Q&A. With a quality pitch, this should be enough time for you to interest investors who want to know more. That's all an initial pitch should do.

In that time, founders have to convey a whole lot of critical information. In Chapter 4, I identified the three characteristics—integrity, determination, and street smarts—that I want to see in the first 45 seconds. This chapter deals with how best to use whatever time you have left.

Before we get into the mechanics of the pitch, let's start with the audience. Angel investors can be demanding. It's vital for you to know something about the mindset of angels. We are really on your side and want you to succeed. However, we know the challenges you are up against. Our initial skepticism drives us to ask tough questions that allow us to better appreciate and believe in what you're doing. Seattle angel investor and venture capitalist Bill Bryant calls this "permission to believe."

I tend to tune out when a founder clicks on a PowerPoint with a lot of words and looks at the screen or, worse, reads what's there. That's so wrong for a number of reasons. First, the attention needs to be on you. So don't do anything to take the audience's attention from where it belongs.

A PRESENTATION IS
LIKE A SHARK

In *Annie Hall*, Woody Allen is breaking up with his girlfriend. "A relationship is like a shark," he tells her. "It has to constantly move forward or it dies. And I think what we got on our hands is a dead shark." Well, presentations are akin to sharks. A pitch must go relentlessly forward, never stop or go backward, or it will die.

Angels want to see a tight progression. Whether you start with a story that sets up the opportunity for the business or the need for the product, or whether you get right into the opportunity or need, start by telling us what you propose to do, why you propose to do it, and how you propose to do it. The presentation has to flow from a natural beginning to a natural conclusion.

"At the very end of the presentation, you want to knock them out of the park," says David S. Rose, my predecessor as chairman of the New York Angels. David gave a celebrated TED conference talk on the art of the pitch to investors that has been viewed over 700,000 times, and I urge you to view it. It's one of the reasons that *Business Week* described David as The Pitch Coach. "You want to be able to get them to such an emotional high that they are ready to write you a check, throw money at you, right there before you leave," he says. But how do you start, and how do you get to such an emotional conclusion?

Angels really want your presentation to have touchstones, or points of reference that the angels can relate to. Perhaps the most powerful touchstone is a reference to a respected industry analyst, journalist, or—best of all—customer who has validated the product. We're always listening for actual—not anticipated—metrics like sales figures or cash flow. Other touchstones might include awards, patents, licenses, or anything else that adds validation to your representations. We're always looking for that permission to believe.

WHAT DELIGHTS ME IN A PRESENTATION

There are lots of books and online resources on how entrepreneurs should pitch to investors. I don't want this to be a comprehensive tutorial on the art of pitching, but I do want to give you a sense of what I look for, what I expect, what delights me, and what turns me off, because I think I'm representative of many angels.

I really want to understand what an entrepreneur's motivation is. This is a long-term relationship we are entering into, and I need to know you have the staying power to sustain the journey. A passion for wealth alone won't do it. Your motivation has to be tempered by something that will survive the many inevitable setbacks. And I want to understand why this startup, versus all the other creative opportunities you may have, is front and center in your life. David Rose listens for something that is just a bit orthogonal to conventional wisdom. I, too, appreciate pitches that leave me slightly off-balance.

In his handout "Secrets of the Pitch Coach," David provides a concise introduction to the Perfect Pitch:

Presentation Flow
The single most important thing in sequencing a presentation is that everything must flow logically from beginning to end, and require no prior knowledge. You do NOT want the audience to have to think AT ALL, which means you need to answer every potential question at exactly the right place, just before the audience would think to ask it. Sounds easy, but 99 percent of presentations don't do it.

The Opening
The world's greatest presentation trainers all agree that the presenter has between thirty and sixty seconds to grab the attention of the audience. To do this, start with NOTHING

on the screen but your company logo, your name and your title. Then, begin with something dramatic and memorable that will have the audience want to follow along with you for the rest of the presentation. This opening can be a personal anecdote, an unusual number, a historic progression, a counter-intuitive fact . . . virtually ANYTHING that will open with a bang and set the mood for the remainder of the presentation.

Context Setting

It is crucial that after the opening, the presenter immediately sets out the context for the rest of the presentation. This should NOT(!) be the agenda for the presentation, but rather should (at least for a venture fundraising pitch) be an extraordinarily concise explanation of what the heck the company does: "We manufacture and sell buggy whips"; "We operate a search engine that finds anything on the Internet"; "We are a global terrorist organization dedicated to overthrowing democracy"; whatever. Consider this to be the picture on the outside of a jigsaw puzzle box, that gives the audience the overall picture into which they can then fit each piece as you deliver it.

The Sequence

The slide/topic sequence for a fundraising pitch is pretty straightforward, and should look something like this:

- Company name and logo and your name and title
- Business overview (context setter)
- Management team
- Market size and pain
- What your product is and does

- Your business model (how you make money)

- Your customers (or the customers you are planning to target)

- How you are going to reach your customers (partnerships, channels, marketing)

- Your competition

- Why you are different, better and have something unique

- The financial overview, showing your revenues and expenses for the next 3 to 4 years

- The funding history of the company, how much you want to raise, and what for

- A review slide of the major points, or a great photo of the product or site

If you follow these suggestions, you're going to have a clean, very Zen-like presentation, which is great for conveying who you are and getting me intellectually and emotionally involved. And speaking of Zen, one of the very best sources for inspiration and advice on state-of-the-art presentations is the book and blog, *PresentationZen*, by Garr Reynolds.

DAVID S. ROSE'S TOP FIVE PRESENTATION TIPS

1. Never, ever look at the screen.

2. Never read your remarks; speak fluidly without notes.

3. Always use Presenter mode so you can see the upcoming slide.

4. Always use a remote control.

5. The handouts you give out are not your presentation. Your slides should have little to no text; instead, make up a special "leave-behind" deck with the text added back in.

SHOW ME YOU'RE IN CONTROL

When I'm being pitched, I like to feel that you're in control. Patrick Ambron, the CEO of BrandYourself, introduced in Chapter 3, is a master of pacing. Entrepreneurs should know their business better than I do; if I believe the founder is likely to get to what I'm interested in, I'm content to hold off interjecting questions for a while. Ambron has learned to apply emotionally intelligent signage to help impatient angels relax: "I'm going to give you a five-minute overview of the product and the business model. I think it will answer all your questions, and then I'll be glad to answer any questions you may still have. So, BrandYourself is . . ."

When you're waiting in a line, you know how reassuring it is to see a sign that indicates how long the wait is? That's emotionally intelligent signage. I appreciate narrative equivalents to such signage in your presentation.

Why would you give a presentation without answering the critical questions you know will be asked? Take control of the situation and anticipate the important questions. The angels will be impressed, and you will come off as more prepared and ready to handle more in-depth follow-up questions.

HOW WILL MY INVESTMENT BE USED?

Many angels want to know how, specifically, their investment will be used. The more concrete and detailed your presentation is on this point, the better. These angels tend to invest when they know that the startup has been thoughtful about how their investment will be applied and that it will move the startup forward in a meaningful way.

If you provide a specific overview of how much money will go toward development, salaries, operations, and marketing, many angels will perk their ears up. Frankly, some angels are sensitive about startups spending too much money on marketing, especially advertising and promotion, and are reluctant to see their money going toward these expenses. We like to believe that you can find more creative viral marketing approaches that cost far less than traditional advertising or marketing.

"The more specific entrepreneurs can be in identifying how the money in the round will be spent and how long it will take them, the better," says my New York Angels colleague Alain Bankier. How will they allocate the funding, how far will it take them, and what is their next milepost: proof of concept, the next round, or the ultimate goal of being cash-flow positive? These are some of the points he expects entrepreneurs to clarify during the course of a presentation.

Angels also want to know that their investment will go to new initiatives and not simply to pay off sunk costs. Bankier focuses on the balance sheet to ensure that his investment will help drive the startup forward. Ideally, that means the money he invests will definitely drive new development, new customer acquisition, new product design. Few angels are enthusiastic about their investment going to pay off "old" costs such as accrued expenses or deferred salaries. You will improve your chances if you specify the productive ways you will use the investment and how the money will incrementally move the startup toward profitability.

START WITH YOURSELF

At this point, you have choices, and I'm open to any course that moves the presentation forward. You can start by introducing the management team. But don't dwell on the team members' backgrounds, as illustrious as they may be. We're more interested in what you're going to do, not what you've done. Remember, I'm drawn to teams that have serial entrepreneurial experience, so if you've previously stewarded one or more businesses from startup to exit, now is definitely the time to mention it.

You can start with the market that is in need of your solution. As you describe your product, remember the last thing I want is the product pitch. I don't care about the features, functions, and benefits. Not now. I just want to know how the product solves a customer problem. I definitely don't want to sit through a live demo, although a very tight video clip is acceptable if it's totally professionally done.

Once I understand what you're selling, I'd like to know how you intend to make money. Tell me why people are excited enough to fork over good money for it. This is the time to get as specific as possible. Do everything you can to back up your assertions. Make me believe the numbers are real. It's okay to admit that you're thinking through various scenarios, and by all means, identify assumptions as assumptions. I just want to know you're intelligently reaching your conclusions. Do your best to describe the business model. Per-unit sales? Freemium? Premium subscription? Advertising? Recurring revenues? Affiliate sales? Whatever. It's always best to have multiple revenue streams.

Most of all, I want to know what the drivers of sales are. Let me see how your business model can translate into reasonable revenue streams.

Tell me something new about the market, and show me you understand you know where the market is, what the demographics are, how to reach the customer segments, and what the costs of doing so will be. Do you have distribution relationships or partnerships that will make reaching customers easier? Do you have a unique competitive advantage? If so, this is a good time to say so.

Sooner rather than later in the pitch, you'll need to present your financials. I realize that early-stage companies don't have a lot or even any historical financial data to present. Fine. Projections more than four years out are just hallucinations, and I've never known anyone to achieve them, but it is reasonable for you to project your first and even second years. This is critical because everyone wants to know when you will achieve break-even or will require additional financing.

VALUATION EXPECTATIONS

Anticipate questions about your startup's valuation. This part of the presentation must be clear and definitive. Are you looking for a priced equity round, or are you looking for convertible debt, which will offer a price capped note and percentage discount on the Series A round? If you have money committed from other sources, we need to know. Who from? On what terms? How much of your own money have you and your team invested?

JUDY ROBINETT'S PRESENTATION TIPS

Judy Robinett is managing director of Golden Seeds, a $40 million angel fund focused on women entrepreneurs. She is an active investor in startups focused on life sciences and high-tech, often taking board positions to guide strategies to market. Any startup requesting funding from Golden Seeds has to have a woman who owns at least 10 percent of the business. If a company doesn't have at least one woman on the board, Robinett wants to know why and has yet to hear a satisfactory response. "The research is clear: there will be an increase in ROI with diversity on the board," she says. "Commitment must start at the top." From 2000 to 2008, Robinett served as CEO of Medical Discoveries, Inc., a publicly traded, developmental biotech venture. Trained as a social worker, Robinett now devotes her energy to consulting on strategic plans and financing for newly emerging companies. If you're going to pitch Judy Robinett, you should certainly do the following:

- **Regard her as you would a customer.** The product you are asking angels to "buy" is you and your company, so they want to know what they will get for their investment. Too many entrepreneurs are so in love with their projects that they forget that money has value. The lesson: describe your funding strategy from where you are now to how much you need to reach certain milestones. With $1 million, maybe you could build infrastructure, hire a team, and secure patents, but to get a revenue stream going, you will need additional rounds of funding. Be conservative about what you promise so that you can meet or beat expectations.

- **Demonstrate that you understand how to get to the next level.** It's less important to posture about the ultimate business than to demonstrate you have a plan to get to the next level. Focus on what it takes to be successful in the short term. Early-stage investing carries great risk, so investors bet mostly on the character of the entrepreneur. It's up to you to show that you value the angels' money and that you want them to act as mentors and to open doors for you.

- **Create a strong customer acquisition model.** Demonstrate that you understand what it costs to acquire a customer. Let the investors know you have done the work of calculating the size of segments and identifying the channels for reaching them. If entrepreneurs say they have no competition, it's safe to assume that there is no market for what they are selling. Ideas are easy; it's execution that counts.

- **Anticipate problems and solutions.** The line between product idea and product launch is never a straight one. Investors want to know you have contingency plans for the most likely disruptions. These "what if?" assumptions show the quality of your thinking. Anybody can produce great spreadsheets with hockey-stick numbers; hitting them is the hard part.

- **Focus on the investor-entrepreneur relationship.** Smart startups understand that the relationship comes first. Numbers alone don't make an investment. Building trust is the key to investor-raising versus money-raising. Angel investing is a small world; word gets around about your integrity. So it's imperative that entrepreneurs be truthful, transparent, and congenial in every aspect. Burning bridges with one investor can cut off multiple sources because of their extensive networks.

MAKE ME SMARTER

Angels are intensely curious, alert to the facts and fast changing trends that are shaping new markets like your own. Knowing about and understanding these changes make me a better investor. I appreciate founders whose pitches provide the following:

- We're going to help educate you about our market.

- Here's our take on what the world will be like in three years.

- Our research indicates the integration in these two markets so that . . .

It's perfectly fine to go out on a limb if you can support your conclusions. That takes confidence and foresight, two qualities I certainly admire.

THE RULES OF SOCIAL MEDIA

Fast Company asked its savviest readers to share some best practices for social media. Many of these also serve as useful guides to shaping presentations, pitching to angels, and even running a business. How does your presentation stack up on these points?

- Would an actual person talk that way?

- The consumer is out for himself, not for you.

- Have an ROI. Have an ROI. Have an ROI.

- Don't make people do X, Y, then Z. Stick with X.

- Your fans own your brand.

- Everyone's an influencer.

- If all you do is respond to complaints, that's all customers will send you.

- As monetization attempts go up, consumer experience goes down.

- If you don't see financial results, you wasted your money.

- Solve problems for people who talk about you, even if they don't address you.

- Not everything will work, and that's fine.

- Offer more value than you expect to get in return.

THE BID FOR ACTION

And then comes the ask, the point of the pitch in the first place. Salespeople call it the "bid for action." There's no sense in being coy. We all know why we're here. Tell me how much money you actually want to raise. You're looking for $500,000? Ask for it and tell me how long it will last.

You should be about done by now. I've probably heard enough to make a decision. Either I'm interested or I'm not. It's better for you to make sure of my intentions since you do not want to lose precious time.

If there are some points I'm curious about, I'll ask you additional questions. If you've done your homework and prepared well, there will be relatively few critical questions left unanswered. But angels like to see how founders think on their feet, so we will probably throw you a question or two. Some of us, unfortunately, just like to hear ourselves speak. So if there's an opportunity for Q&A, you will certainly get it.

It's time to wrap up. I hope I'm as enthusiastic and excited as you are. I love nothing better than the shared experience of hearing something great presented in a way that really makes sense. Make an emotional connection and conclude with a final pitch. You should make time for a concluding statement that ties it all together and hurls me into orbit with your startup at the center.

PITCHING TURNOFFS

There are lots of ways to get me cranky when you're pitching.

- **Saying "unique" and "revolutionary."** As an old PR/marketing guy, I know nothing is further from the truth than saying something is "unique" or "revolutionary." Let your audience be the judge after you've made your case and presented an exhaustive market analysis.

- **Shooting from the hip.** Angels hate BS. "I'd rather hear an honest 'I don't know' than a desperate attempt to make up something on the spot," says angel investor Alain Bankier. Other appropriate responses when you don't know: "Let me get back to you on that" or "We haven't resolved that yet." And then get back to them in a timely and responsive manner.

- **Using loose numbers.** You have to know your numbers cold. Own the vital signs of your company. I want to understand in detail how much your product costs, the costs of every component, how much it costs to make it, as well as how much it costs to make a sale. You can't punt on this or delegate. When I first heard the pitch from Tom Patterson, the founder of Tommy John Underwear, I was impressed by his command of the numbers and ultimately invested in his reinvention of men's underwear. He understood his financials, margins, the P&L, the balance sheet. "There are good businesses and great businesses," Patterson says, "but the great entrepreneurs are in total command of their financials. This task can't be delegated. Anyone can have a great idea, but true entrepreneurs don't ask others to do something they haven't done themselves."

- **Inconsistency.** If you tell me you expect sales of your product to be $2 million and then, 10 slides later, the number is $2.5 million, I'm going to wonder if it's a typo, or maybe one number is gross sales and the other net sales. In any case, you've lost me. It doesn't reassure me to worry about the meaning of the most basic numbers in your presentation.

- **Confusing me.** Anything that makes me scratch my head will stop the flow of the presentation. By all means, take me through all the steps, but if you leave out a step that may be obvious to you, you'll leave me behind, and I'll need to figure out the missing steps. Frankly, I don't want to work that hard.

- **Keeping a day job while running a startup.** I want to invest in founders who have the confidence and commitment to put everything they have into the venture. Hedging your bets by keeping your job tells me that you're not ready to accept the risks of a startup. I won't think less of you for that. Having a steady income and benefits is a personal decision. But if you're not ready to commit full time to the startup, I am not ready to invest.

- **Sloppiness.** I'm pretty hard on presentations with typos, misspellings, mistakes in addition, or a table out of place. I worry that if you can't even get a presentation right, how will you run a company?

- **Arguing between founders.** It's just so middle school to witness a pitch in which the founders are correcting each other or arguing among themselves. You'd be surprised how often it happens.

- **Urgency.** Dating and pitching have a lot in common. You can't expect to turn a blind date into a marriage proposal in one go-around. Now, I haven't dated in a long time, but as I recall, the point of a date is to get to know each other and determine suitability for moving forward. Promises matter less than the confidence that comes from just exchanging stories. So it is in the dance between entrepreneur and angel investor. I want to get to know you gradually and by talking determine for myself if you can deliver on your promises. What I want to see, more than anything else, is energy that burns bright. By all means, show me your commitment to success, but urgency is always counterproductive.

- **Mistaking me for a customer.** I'm a potential investor, not a customer. Don't ask me to sit through a product demo. Too many entrepreneurs are so in love with their products that they want to evangelize about them instead of recognizing what they should be selling: the concept and the team. The product that I am buying is you and your team.

The product you are so currently excited about will almost certainly be something else by the time you launch.

Howard Morgan, founder of First Round Capital, says it's a basic mistake for entrepreneurs to confuse an investor with a customer. "When you are making your pitch, you're selling multiple things," Morgan advises, "but to investors you are making a pitch to buy your shares." The clearer founders are about what investors are actually buying, the better they can craft the pitch about what it is they are selling.

- **Nepotism.** I'm not going to invest in founder teams that include boyfriends and girlfriends or lovers of any gender. Do I have to explain why? Next! I get nervous when I see relatives on the team, especially if they have invested in the company. Is your brother-in-law really the best developer available? Yes, you need a lawyer, but—as competent and reasonably priced as he may be—it shouldn't be your father. Doing a startup is complicated enough without the added complexity of dealing with romantic interests or relatives on the payroll. I've seen such arrangements blow up and threaten entire enterprises. Keep it simple as much as you can. When you hire, cast the net wide to find the very best person for each role.

- **Talking about "sales."** Sales are so last century. Nobody wants to be sold to. If you have business cards with the word "sales" on them, throw them away. You want to be on the same side of the table as your customer.

STARTUP ENTREPRENEURS, TRANSLATED

When startup entrepreneurs talk, angel investors listen. But what do angels really hear and think?

What they said. "We have an incredible, game-changing, transformational vision for the future."
What we heard. "We have our heads in the clouds with little idea how to execute."

What they said. "We haven't finalized that data yet."
What we heard. "That data doesn't make sense."

What they said. "We're staying on message because our strategy is in line with our values."
What we heard. "We like to talk about ourselves."

What they said. "We are in it for the long haul. We are not looking for a quick sell."
What we heard. "No one is stupid enough to buy us."

What they said. "We're pursuing a blue ocean strategy."
What we heard "We don't have a clue what our strategy is."

What they said. "This is all very new and exciting."
What we heard. "Do you have any advice? We could really use some advice."

What they said. "Our financials are conservative."
What we thought. "Even so, they'll never make those numbers."

What they said. "We're 'Facebook for X.'"
What we thought. "Great, yet another one."

What they said. "All we need is a 1 percent market share, and we'll all be billionaires."
What we thought. "They have no clue how much customer acquisition will cost."

What they said. "BigNameVC is really interested in us."
What we thought. "Anybody can express interest. Who's writing you checks?"

YOU WANT ME TO SIGN AN NDA?
FORGET IT!

Almost no experienced investor will sign a nondisclosure agreement (NDA), so don't ask. Doing so marks you as a rank amateur.

Instead of protecting your precious idea, you should be shouting it from the rooftops to everyone who will listen. This includes investors, of course, but also friends, family, neighbors, the hairdresser, and the guy next to you in line at Starbucks. Don't worry about people stealing it. First of all, most people will think your idea is worthless. That does not mean your idea really is without value. It's actually a good sign when your idea challenges the conventional wisdom. If everyone loved your idea, I'd tell you it's not disruptive enough.

The risk of someone stealing your precious idea is essentially zero. Have you ever met anyone who is willing to drop everything they're doing to copy an untested idea? Would you? It just doesn't happen. People are too busy pursuing their own ideas. As for angel investors, we're in the business of funding existing teams and ideas. We have absolutely no interest in building untested companies around the countless untested ideas that come our way.

So spread the word about your idea as widely as possible. Tweet and blog about it. By doing so, you get to gauge people's excitement level. You get to refine your elevator pitch. You get to discover wrinkles and flaws you haven't considered. You might even hear about a competing product that makes your idea irrelevant. If you do, consider yourself lucky. By being open with your idea, you've just saved yourself years of fruitless work and expense.

CHAPTER 5 TAKEAWAYS

- Traction leads to attention.

- Put something out on the Web or Kickstarter to see if it gets traction.

- Use trusted referrals from LinkedIn, Facebook, or other social media connections.

- Don't cold e-mail. It's usually a waste of time.

- Develop a 30-second elevator pitch, and look for opportunities to present it at events attended by investors.

- Don't ask an angel to sign an NDA.

- Identify what you intend to do with the angel's investment.

Every Business
Starts with a Belief

Every startup begins with a belief, and I want to know what that belief is. It's not as simple a question as you may think. Quick: what's the belief that inspires your startup?

When I say that every startup begins with a belief, most entrepreneurs nod their heads in immediate recognition. Pursuits always begin with a belief. Whether it's a startup, an art project, a philanthropic cause, an invention, or social change, the belief always comes first. Some of the pursuits succeed and some fail, but I've never seen a pursuit fail because the belief was too big. When pursuits fail, it's almost always because the execution is too small.

Whose beliefs are we talking about? The entrepreneurs', to be sure. But angel investors start with a belief, too.

The entrepreneur starts with a belief in the power of a new product or service. The angel starts with a belief in the startup, which is another way of saying that the angel has a belief in the founder(s). The beliefs are intertwined. But at the start, most angel investors are less interested in the market merits of your belief than in the qualities of your belief system and your ability to execute.

These are some of the questions I need you to answer:

- What is the basis of your belief system?

- What do you believe about the nature of your world that causes you to have such confidence in your idea?

- Is your belief based on some personal insight?

- Have you identified a behavior that needs to be adapted and changed?

- Have you arrived at your insight through analytical analysis?

- Can you execute on this belief?

Paul Saffo, managing director of foresight at Discern Analytics and an expert on the dynamics of long-term change, said, "Don't confuse a clear view for a short distance." Just because something seems terribly obvious and necessary doesn't mean it's going to happen quickly or at all. A startup needs a belief, but the belief needs to be open to quick implementation.

When founders believe something, the belief shines though in every facet of their presentation. It's like a riff in music; you hear it over and over again throughout the score. It represents more than the passion to build something. It means the founders have taken the time to challenge a set of established practices or attitudes, often in the analog world, that can be repurposed by a new set of practices or attitudes. Often the unifying principles are to eliminate asymmetries of information, reduce costs, increase market efficiency, and generally decrease friction. But in the end, I believe it's about human behaviors. You can talk all you want about the business stuff, but in the end it's all about understanding human behaviors and figuring out how to give people what they need faster, smarter, and perhaps even cheaper.

Do I invest only in high-tech? No, but it's hard to imagine any business today where technology does not provide some critical leverage.

BELIEF + EXECUTION = SUCCESS

Yes, I need to believe in the belief, but I also need to believe in the execution. After I hear about the belief and the startup it inspired, my next questions revolve around the theme, "I wonder how they will execute?"

A Big Hairy Belief is of little or no value until it's put into motion. I'm skeptical of startups that bring me a plateful of ideas generated by brainstorming or crowdsourcing. Maybe some of the ideas have merit, but the startup won't know until it has subjected the lot to what Bob Killian of Killian Branding calls "crap-sifting," in which a skilled editor can perhaps extract a valuable nugget capable of execution.

As much as I like Big Beliefs, I'll take great execution every time. Give me perfect execution of a decent-sized idea over imperfect execution of a big idea. Too many founders get self-satisfied by the elegance of their Big Beliefs and fail to roll up their sleeves to figure out how to do the down and dirty labor that actually transforms a concept into a business. It's the determination to execute flawlessly that transforms founders into successful entrepreneurs. I don't want founders to be entrepreneurs; I want them to be successful entrepreneurs.

Too many startup teams disintegrate under the withering questions angels ask about execution: "How do you define a unit, and what are the corresponding unit economics?" "What's the cost for customer acquisition?" "What do you expect the burn rate to be?" Are you ready for such questions?

I recall the 2010 Angel Capital Association conference in Boston when Timothy "Scott" Case, the CEO of Startup America

Partnership, got up to speak. He couldn't have been more excited to get in front of 500 of the most check-writing angel investors in the world. He began by talking about his enthusiasm to address such a distinguished crowed. "We need more angel investors in the world," he said.

"No, you don't!" said a member of the audience.

Startled, Case shielded his eyes against the glare of the lights and scanned the audience. "Who said that?"

"I did," said a gentleman, standing up. He was one of the most respected members of the angel investing community, so he was not to be dismissed.

"Say what you mean," Case said.

"The world doesn't need more angel investors," the man said. "The world needs smarter angel investors."

Everyone nodded. Too many unsophisticated angels means too many down rounds, too many frustrated entrepreneurs, and too many disappointed angels. Stewarding startups to funding is difficult and requires angels with a real commitment to the task. The subtitle of this book refers to "smart funding" in honor of the angel who stood up that day. One of the goals of this book is to demonstrate that smart funding pursuing smart investments creates the optimum conditions for success for both startups and the angels who fund them.

YOUR IDEA IS NOT AS IMPORTANT AS YOU THINK IT IS

Perhaps the most common mistake founders make is to believe every great startup requires a Big Idea, and that with a Big Idea, they will have no trouble securing financing. I wish it were that simple, because I'd love to live in a world guided by indispensable Big Ideas. But for better or for worse, that's not the world we live in.

Some founders assume that if a business is profitable, it is fundable. Not so. Not all profitable startups are good investments for angels. Angels fund only businesses that are scalable, with the expectation of financial returns. We often are asked to invest in lifestyle businesses, such as restaurants, retail stores, or personal service businesses. These may be fine, profitable businesses, but they are simply not fundable. Such businesses are typically too labor-intensive to allow the scalability angels require. Nor do they offer the opportunity for a decent exit that angels need to make up for the large number of losses we historically have.

Another mistake that founders make is trying to get funding for startups with long sales cycles followed by long implementation periods. Startups can't afford the time—not with a typical burn rate of $200,000 per month. You'll be bled to death before you get paid.

I see a lot of Big Ideas that take my breath away by their sheer inspiration and chutzpah. I love the energy and passion that entrepreneurs and their Big Ideas generate. And I accept that the boundless optimistic energy of entrepreneurs is necessary to sustain the innovation and creation of a business. But the reality is that Big Ideas, by themselves, do not determine success, and they do not, by themselves, secure financing.

There is a growing number of what I call "Hollywood" angels who are easily impressed by shiny Big Ideas who you can probably convince to give you money. Unfortunately, these angels are quite binary in their investments. It's either a big hit or it's not. This has led to poorly thought out valuations, which at the start may excite the founders but turn out to hurt the company and the initial investors, because it's so hard to achieve the expected financial goals. This leads to down rounds of financing that crush the entrepreneur and the initial investors.

"Don't overstructure the deal," says Manuel Henriquez, CEO of Hercules Technology Growth Capital of Palo Alto, California, a specialty financing company that provides debt financing to pre-IPO, venture-backed companies. He reminds angel investors that it's called "risk capital" for a reason. "If you're doing angel investment, accept that you may take some losses. Don't oversaddle the startup with an unrealistic valuation that will make it impossible for the founder to secure additional financing," Henriquez says.

Not every great company requires a Big Idea. Starbucks' success is based not on unique coffee but on the underwhelming idea that customers would find the hangout atmosphere of its stores and the Starbucks baristas welcoming. Zappos is a great shoe retailer not because it sells better shoes but because it sells shoes better.

Some angels question the whole vision thing. Angel investor Linda Holliday sees a lot of startups based on ideas that are attractive but don't really aspire to a grand vision: "If you believe there's a better way to make change at cash registers, I might back you, but 'vision' feels like a big word for something so transactional."

When entrepreneurs start talking to me about their Big Ideas, I listen. Then I ask questions. First of all, is the Big Idea really new? Has no one in human history thought of it before? It's more likely that with a little digging, you will discover someone somewhere who indeed came up with the same idea and rejected it for reasons you will likely discover for yourself.

Combining a big vision and the ability to execute with precision isn't for the faint of heart. But then neither is life. If you truly want your startup to reach its full potential, embrace the belief, but let the belief be the starting point of a detailed, step-by-step plan that you can flawlessly execute.

Your belief doesn't have to be in the digital media space, either. While much of my investing is indeed in the digital world, and while social media is driving much of the startup economy, there are plenty of entrepreneurs who have impressed me with their beliefs and who are building traditional analog enterprises. What, for example, could be more traditional than retail men's underwear?

UNDERSTAND UNDERWEAR

Tom Patterson had a belief about men's underwear. He believed that most underwear for men sucked, that none of the incredible innovation in women's undergarments had migrated to men's underwear. And he believed he absolutely knew how to make men's underwear better. Before meeting Tom, I certainly didn't give much thought to my underwear, but after listening to him for just a few minutes, I was ready to underwrite the revolution in men's underwear that Tom was proposing.

Tom has basically reinvented men's underwear. So the first lesson is that not all startups are cloud-based, social media plays. The second point is that Tom really made me work for the right to invest in Tommy John. You should also know that prior to starting his company, Tom worked as a medical device salesman.

I first saw Tom's pitch at the New York Angels and was hugely impressed. After his presentation, I told him that I was interested and that he should call me. Some weeks later, I was having a drink with a fellow angel when Tom called. I was at this little bar that served a variety of craft beers and was at the feeling-good end of a flight of brews. "So, Brian, you said you want to invest in my company," Tom said. "Tell me about yourself. Tell me why should I take money from you."

It was a very direct question, and it sobered me up straight away. There I was, outside a bar on the Lower East Side, trying to sell myself to a guy who had an idea to improve underwear. I don't remember exactly what I said, but my lasting impression is that I was fascinated by the direct way he wanted to know everything about me.

I think most angels have outsized egos. I've been told I do, and there's plenty of evidence for confirmation. I believe that most angels would react positively, as I did, to Tom's questions. We all secretly want to share, in detail, what makes us special. I appreciated his questions about how I could help him realize his dream. I do remember one question he asked: "Can you be committed to me?" Such a powerful question. And my answer was, "Absolutely." And I am—I am totally committed to Tom Patterson. Now I almost always wear Tommy John underwear.

Tom's story is instructive. He was raised in Milbank, South Dakota, a small town in which his father owned a funeral parlor, furniture store, and ambulance service. Entrepreneurialism came easily to young Tom, and he started a number of small enterprises such as lawn mowing and snow plowing while he was in high school. He told anyone who would ask that his goal was to build a successful brand from the ground up. Upon graduating from Arizona State University, he took a conventional job as a medical device salesman, but he was always restless for his chance.

Tom got into the retail business by accident. He was a fervid fan of the old MSNBC show *The Big Idea*, hosted by Donny Deutsch. "I was always impressed by people who could turn ideas into products and businesses," Tom recalls. "What I loved about the show was that Deutsch would insist that the inventors go through all the steps: 'Okay, you got the idea, then what? You made the product, then what?'" Tom realized that what many of the successful products had in common was that they improved on existing products. "I came to realize that most people were frustrated by limitations or deficiencies in the products they used," he says. On his commute to work, Tom kept asking himself what products in his own life needed improvement.

One day, he got out of his car after a long commute to go into a hospital for another sales presentation. He noticed that his undershirt had risen up and bunched around his waist. During his pitch to the New York Angels, when Tom mentioned this moment, every man in the room inspected his waist for what Tom calls EFG (excess fabric gut)—that shapeless bump just above the belt line caused by a loose-fitting undershirt. I could relate to what Tom was saying, because the same thing frustrates me.

There in the hospital parking lot, the vision for Tommy John was born. "Why can't someone make an undershirt that won't rise up?" Tom asked himself. He thought about how badly his undershirts fit and how quickly they lost their shape. Men's undershirts were designed like Band-Aids, he realized— almost disposable. A quick trip to the shopping mall confirmed his hunch: no one made undershirts that were really fitted to avoid EFG.

About this time, fate forced Tom's hand. It was 2008, during the financial crisis. Tom was laid off from his medical sales job. From watching *The Big Idea*, Tom understood that there is no better time to start a business than during a recession. He decided to go for it:

> Instead of going back to corporate America, I did everything you're not supposed to do. I depleted my savings account, I cashed out my 401(k), I relied on my friends at American Express. I decided never to be the coulda/shoulda/woulda guy who regretted what might have been. I thought, "Gosh, I have a product that every one of the 65 percent of men in America who wear undershirts needs." I knew I could always get another medical sales job."

In the following weeks, Tom worked to refine his idea. He drove to Los Angeles and bought $100 worth of a light fabric with stretch and recovery characteristics that he thought would make a good undershirt. Then, with his rudimentary drawing skills, he sketched out a pattern for an undershirt. He took the sketch to the tailor at his dry cleaner and asked if he could sew an undershirt based on the pattern. The tailor's response: "Why do you want to waste all this great fabric on an undershirt?" But he said he would sew it.

Tom tried the shirt on and was delighted. No more EFG. His undershirt didn't ride up even on long commutes, and even after numerous washings, they kept their fit much longer than conventional undershirts by Hanes, Jockey, or Fruit of the Loom. After more research, he developed a patent-pending fabric that is soft and super-wickable with properties similar to cotton but that resists shrinkage and yellowing. Tom was personally pleased with the results, but could he get his friends interested?

He ordered up 15 more shirts and gave them to men he trusted to provide him with authentic feedback. Tom intuitively understood something I tell all the founders I mentor: it's very hard to get authentic criticism. Everyone, especially those closest to the founder, wants to be supportive, not realizing the most supportive thing to do is to be absolutely candid.

Tom called his friends and said, "Hey, I'm gonna send you some undershirts. I need to know if they are good." Their response was predictable: "All right, Tom, whatever." Well, a few days went by, and Tom started to hear back from his friends. They all said, "Wow! These are great. Can I get four or five more?" Tom said, "Gimme a month." Encouraged, Tom went to Los Angeles, found a manufacturer, and commissioned a lot of 200 undershirts based on his design and fabric. He sold that first lot and used the money to commission 500 more and to build a website. And that's how Tom's business got started. When I met him, he already had a small online retail presence and some wildly enthusiastic customers.

With positive reviews in hand, Tom relocated to California and founded Tommy John. Tom's big break came when he secured a meeting with a buyer at Niemen Marcus, which tested the undershirts in three stores. Sales exceeded expectations, and soon every Niemen Marcus was stocking Tommy John men's underwear. High-end retailers Nordstrom and Saks followed in short order. Tom outsourced the manufacturing to China, where the margins were better, and relocated the company to New York, the fashion capital of the world, where he felt the brand would most prosper.

Tom's first presentation to the New York Angels came in September 2011. We invited him back two months later. The differences between the presentations were striking. Says Tom,

> Everything takes longer. You pitch and revise. The second pitch forced me to dig even more into the financials, the P&L, the balance sheet. I knew the numbers, but I didn't know them as well as I should have known them. Founders really need to understand the margins. The New York Angels really pushed me on the math over and over again. Eventually, you connect with someone who believes in you. Things align when they are meant to be.

As an investor, I liked that Tom had a successful sales background. To me, that meant he could articulate a value proposition and, more important, that he knew what it takes to make sales calls happen. I was also impressed by one of Tom's "aha" moments. Tom describes the experience in his own words:

> Shortly after my product was accepted by Niemen Marcus, I learned that the sales managers of each department gather all the sales associates for a short "morning rally" in which they review the sales numbers of the previous day, note the day's sales and promotions, and go over selling points or "collateral" to move the merchandise. I was invited to attend one of these meetings and was totally surprised when the sales manager turned to me and said, "By the way, we have Tom Patterson, the founder of Tommy John underwear, here. Tom, can you come up and say a few words?"
> I had no idea I would be called on to say anything. Luckily my sales training kicked in, and I stammered a few details about the product and its features. Well, that department sold more Tommy John undershirts that day than ever before. So I started asking—begging—to speak at as many

morning rallies as possible, and each time I did, the sales numbers—and subsequent orders—would go up. Whenever I visit a city, I beg for the opportunity to speak before the sales associates.

As for funding, six months into the project, Tom got about $100,000 from a friend who loved the product and offered to invest. I came along when Tommy John already had a proven niche brand, sustainable revenues, a distribution network, and growing market share. I tried the product, and now I swear by it. There's no going back to Hanes when you've tried briefs from Tommy John. I'm a proud investor. Revenue in 2012 was $5 million, up from $1.5 million in 2011.

Having updated the undershirt, Tommy John turned its attention to men's undershorts. "We don't develop a problem unless we can solve a problem," Tom says. "Women's underwear is like the Jetsons, futuristic, innovative, and fun. But underwear for men hasn't been modernized in generations." The upshot of Tom's innovation? A men's brief with fabric that stretches and rotates in all directions instead of just up and down, or left and right. Plus, as promised, it solves the problem of briefs riding up the wearer's thighs. The biggest innovation: a "quick-draw" fly that is oriented not vertically but horizontally. The briefs even have a pocket for an iPod.

Looking back on it, it wasn't the quick-draw fly or the iPod pocket that impressed me most. It was the utter simplicity of Tom's belief that he was uniquely positioned to reinvent men's underwear. He had thought the situation through. With his experiments, he demonstrated so much with so little. His interest in solving the underwear problem wasn't partial. It was complete.

Tom is what I call a visionary. His belief led him to see things that others didn't and to create a solution to a problem that people didn't recognize as a problem with a solution. I mean, I've long been frustrated at my undershirts jamming up around my waist, but I just accepted it. People who invent the future see things that we don't see; they have deep beliefs in the way things should be and undertake to change the status quo to make them better.

FIVE BELIEFS I'D LIKE
EVERY STARTUP TO HAVE

To launch a startup, entrepreneurs must make thousands of decisions. If they get even a third of those important decisions right, they're geniuses. There are no guarantees, but decisions inspired by these five beliefs will go a long way to getting it right the first time.

1. **The team we have is ideal.** Business models and product specs are easy to change. The hardest thing to change is the mix of partners. There are no hard and fast rules about how to do this, but a long history usually is a good sign. I love it when I see a melodic and fluid conversation between founders.

2. **We believe in launching sooner rather than later.** A startup hasn't really started working until its product or service has been launched. Research and focus groups are fine. But nothing educates a startup about what it should be developing until something is injected into the marketplace.

3. **We understand our customers.** I'm impressed by founders who work harder at asking intelligent questions than at answering them. The best startups understand their customers sometimes better than their customers understand themselves.

4. **We are committed to metrics and analytics.** The simple act of measuring something has an uncanny tendency to improve it. Of course, measurement is rarely simple. It's easy to measure the wrong things. I like startups to have a belief

in measurement and the discipline to be guided by what the metrics reveal and then to adapt as quickly as possible.

5. **We believe in being frugal.** The reality is that most startups fail before they can deliver a product or service that customers are willing to pay for. What happens is that the startups run out of money. I want to see a culture of frugality in everything the startup touches.

JAXX: A MESSAGING PLATFORM FOR MEN

In this book's introduction, I promised to tell you about the winners of the first Boston College Venture Competition (BCVC), which awarded $10,000 in honor of my mentor, the late Professor Harold G. Buchbinder. The winners were a team led by Boston University MBA candidate Phil Mark. His iPhone application is a male-only social network ("where guys go to be guys") called Jaxx that is designed to help men stay in touch. Phil's big insight is that unlike women, who want to socialize over shared information and feelings, men prefer to engage by sharing sports, drinking, and other guy bonding stuff.

Like virtually all startups, Jaxx did not emerge fully formed. The product that Phil first submitted was a location-based application called MineGames. I was among the judges of the business plan competition and came away impressed less by the game than by the founder. Cofounder Phil Mark recounts the team's experience with me:

> We were so green. Brian helped us narrow down the problem we wanted to solve. He wanted us to talk to many more people and do a lot more user research. The questions Brian asked helped us think deeply about the value we were adding to the user. In MineGames was embedded the idea for

what we really wanted to do with Jaxx, and he helped us identify it, extract it, and polish it for the world.

Through Jaxx, guys can create a private circle of friends and then send group messages about various activities or events going on in their area. Men can also create challenges for individual friends or an entire group, whether it be betting on a poker tournament or a lifting event. Popular is the "suggest a plan" feature, which allows guys to either accept or decline invitations for a proposed night out. A "roast" function allows guys to leave geonotes out in the world for their friends—essentially a clever "What's up?" that can be opened when friends arrive at the tagged location.

When I first met the Jaxx team, they were barely past the inspiration stage. Phil Mark recalls what he learned from that early stage of the startup process:

> Expose your thought process to as many people as early on as possible. You need all the feedback. Find advisors who will really challenge you by asking why. Why are you doing that? Why do you think the customer will buy that feature? Why is that of value? Value for whom? Entrepreneurs must connect with their customers. You have to get out of the office, talk to customers, and get the product in their hands.
>
> The most valuable asset you have is time. Really focus on people who care about time and can help you use it best. Once we got confident about what the value proposition was, that's when we made our greatest progress. Oftentimes the feedback you get will be neutral or positive. You really have to seek out people who are confident enough to tell you where you are off or where you lost your way.
>
> Build relationships with investors. In order to secure funding from angels, an entrepreneur needs to establish relationships with potential investors, provide metrics

by which the entrepreneur will be held accountable, and deliver. To my regret, there were early connections we made that I did not nurture because I thought they weren't interested in our product. What they were interested in was the team and seeing what product we would eventually build.

Most startups hit snags, and Jaxx was no exception. Just as this book was going to press, Phil told me that the team was putting the development of Jaxx on hold "for the time being." The team ran short of the funding required to maintain a full-time commitment to the startup. I was sorry to receive the news. When Phil Mark made his Boston University presentation, he was the hands-down winner.

I worked closely with Phil and the team he pulled together, but in the end I chose not to invest. I had to two concerns. First of all, I didn't think the startup had the right team in place. There were redundancies within the team. As CEO, Phil recognized this problem but hesitated to make the tough decisions the situation required. It's hard to unravel a startup team that isn't working; that's why it's so important to get it right from the beginning. But if a correction needs to be made, it should be done quickly. The startup environment is unforgiving of those who waste time, and Phil took too long to make the tough decision.

The other reason I didn't invest is because I simply wasn't convinced that the team really understood its customers, nor could the team articulate why those customers would demand Jaxx in their lives. When I offered them some points to consider, they seemed enthusiastic, but nothing changed. In the end, I concluded that the Jaxx team was like a lot of startups that I see. They mistook a product for a company. They got lost in building something cool and forgot an important lesson: cool may get attention, but it doesn't mean there's a business to be scaled and funded.

CHAPTER 6 TAKEAWAYS

- Know what the belief behind your business is.

- Be prepared to articulate it.

- Belief + Execution = Success.

- Your idea is not as important as you think it is.

- Expose your thought process to as many people as early on as possible.

Investor Raising
vs. Money Raising

Some people talk about "smart money" versus "dumb money." I don't think those terms are particularly helpful. I much prefer thinking about the issue in terms of "investor raising" versus "money raising."

It's tempting for founders to grab whatever funding from whatever source they can. And I understand the limited choices some founders face. Money is money, they say, so grab it—and as much of it as you can. But smart founders gravitate toward smart investors. Money may be fungible, but that doesn't mean that all investors are the same.

Think about it this way. It's not the money that really helps you. It's your choice about the investors who will provide the money, as well as everything else a smart investor offers a startup over the course of its development. Money comes and goes (usually goes), but smart investors tend to stick around. It's the source of the money who can provide counsel, contacts, and other benefits that in long-term value will dwarf the initial monetary investment.

Investor raising is an ongoing process that persists beyond the funding event. Once you have angels on board, you have this incredible opportunity to harvest their knowledge, experience, and network of contacts. I encourage you to start off by making it clear that you are into investor raising, that you want to take advantage of all that they have to offer.

Most angels welcome such an appeal. Many have relevant experience, and most have large networks of people who can be very useful to your startup, both pre- and post-launch.

IT'S NOT EASY TO TURN DOWN MONEY

I know it's tough for startups. It looks like a buyer's market, and you often feel desperate to say yes to anyone who waves dollar bills in front of you. But desperation rarely leads to good outcomes. Angels never want to see your neediness. In fact, the more we are persuaded that you really don't need our money, the more eager some of us are to give it to you.

You ever see the film *Broadcast News*? There's a great line from the hapless TV anchor played by Albert Brooks, whose self-doubt turns him into a flop-sweat basket case when he's on air. He says, "Wouldn't this be a great world if insecurity and desperation made us more attractive? If 'needy' were a turn-on?"

But it isn't, not if you want your investors to put out.

Investor raising means setting up the conditions for a true partnership. The relationship between a founder and an angel is like a professional marriage. Like a marriage, the partners share assets. The investor owns a piece of your company. To the extent you envision your company as an extension of yourself, you are selling a portion of yourself to the investor, who will be your partner, for better or for worse, for richer or for poorer. Ideally, that's what sharing equity means. You're in it together for the long run.

You both hope the long run looks good. If the equity in the union grows, both parties get to share in the bounty. If it doesn't, you both lose. It's when things aren't going so well that you really need each other, and you know that the angels will be there for you. Think about this. Can you see yourself figuratively being in bed with your investor for the next nine years? That's the length of time before the average startup gets a liquidity event. And that's why it's important for you to decide what kind of partner you are willing to accept.

Investor raising is worth its weight in gold. "It's true that money itself isn't dumb or smart," says Dan Kador, CTO of Keen IO. "The judgments attach to the investors behind the money." It's not a question of intelligence, he says, but the ability of investors to materially help advance the startup above and beyond the capital. "Although Keen IO has some investors who haven't shown a desire to actively participate in the startup, they are people we can go to with specific questions and be blown away by the quality of their responses," Kador says. Every Keen IO investor was selected on the basis of his or her unique ability to assist the startup in its growth and evolution. "That's what we call smart money," Kador says.

DO YOU WRITE CHECKS?

When you meet with me or any angel investor, I want you to remember that you are on a sales call. You are selling your startup. And like every sales call, you have to know that a close is possible, that the angel has the ability to write you a check. This is a question of using your time wisely. You have to know that these are serious investors.

The most important thing you should look for in angels is their historical ability to actually write checks. So at a suitable point in the conversation, ask the question: "Do you write checks?"

That's how to keep it real. You're in control. It's remarkable how many angels are tire kickers or dilettantes with a liquidity problem. They will meet with you and ask a hundred questions but never quite get around to closing the deal. So you have to ask the closing question.

Yes, some angels will be taken aback by that. But it's an appropriate closing question; many angels will be impressed by your salesmanship, a skill that predicts success for the startup. They will respect your time management, too.

"If they're not going to write a check, then you are wasting your time, and time is really the only thing of value a startup has," says angel investor Linda Holliday. She believes that in a perfect world, angels should volunteer that they are not interested the minute they determine they are not going to invest. Moreover, she believes that investors owe entrepreneurs a reason why they are not going to invest. I respect the hell out of Linda for this position. You can hear more about Linda's values in Chapter 14.

But let's assume the angels are taken aback by the question. So what? It's likely they don't have checkbooks in their back pockets. Tick tock. Time to move on.

If the angel says yes, the next question follows: "Tell me about the investments you have personally made in the past three months."

When you can muster the confidence to do due diligence on the angel, it signals that you have singular pride in the business you're building. I can tell you that such pride, if backed up by the real thing, inspires angels to get on board. Angels are rarely engaged in this manner. It signals your startup is special and that as the founder, you have a real handle, real control, and real belief in what you are building.

Then you are ready for the only closing question that matters: "We'd like you to participate in our round. Will you invest in our startup?"

Tom Patterson, the founder of Tommy John underwear, asked me an outstanding variant of that question. As I described in Chapter 6, when I heard Tom make a presentation on how he reinvented men's underwear, I was hooked. Later Tom called me and said, "Why I should take money from you?"

I was pleased by the fact that he wanted more than just money from me; he wanted an investor partner. This was different than just responding to some e-mail questionnaire. Tom was listening carefully about how I thought I was the right guy to invest in his business.

Smart investors are active investors. These investors tend to be high-wealth businesspeople whose wealth flows from their success as entrepreneurs, usually from a liquidity event. They are eager to devote both time and money to their portfolios of invested companies. Funding from the best angel investors is smart money. The more you get to know angels, the more targeted you can be. Ideally, you want angel investors who bring with them a set of experiences, skills, and contacts relevant to your industry. Many entrepreneurs report that the time and counsel angels provide their companies is more valuable to them than the initial money.

MEET ANGEL INVESTOR JEFF PULVER

I've said that every angel investor is different. No angel is more different or gets better results than Jeffrey L. Pulver. Jeff is a New York–based entrepreneur (he started the company that became Vonage), thought leader (VoIP), and angel investor (he was an early investor in Twitter). Jeff modestly calls his investment in Twitter "pure luck." He is currently focusing his investment efforts on preseed opportunities in startups in New York City and Israel.

Jeff has invested in over 200 startups and has had a respectable number of exits. A number of the companies he has invested in have grown into significant operating companies and continue to thrive today. His sweet spot is the earliest possible moment of the startup's creation. He prefers to be the first person in whenever possible. Jeff has been known to sit in on high school business plan competitions to look for startup ideas to fund.

What I love about Jeff Pulver in his angel role is how optimistic and people-centered his investing is. "The best gift you can give entrepreneurs is to believe in them," he says. "So I actively look for people to believe in. It's people first, ideas second." Jeff, like me, is an angel investor in order to make the world a little better. "Investing in startups is an amazingly noble effort to change the world, and everyone that does a startup should have that chance," he says.

So what kind of entrepreneurs does Jeff look for? "Life is a series of micropivots. I look for people who are dynamic and flexible," he says, adding that every successful company is successful not for what it plans to do but for what it ends up doing successfully.

When he encounters someone he likes, he tends to say yes. This is "do diligence," Pulver-style. (See Chapter 10 for my take on *due* diligence versus *do* diligence.) For Jeff, conventional due diligence in a paint-by-the-numbers sense is a total waste of time. "Business plans and projections are total fantasies," he says, "and I've never seen a spreadsheet worth anything." Instead Jeff relies on his gut as he looks for some proof of concept and proof of competence. "Does the team have the dynamic ability to look around the corner, run fast, and break through walls or shift direction?" he asks.

A process does inform his judgment. For example, for startups in the digital world, he always wants to confirm that someone on the team is writing the code. Pulver will not fund a startup that intends to use his money to outsource development or prototyping. "I'm looking for a team that's whole," he says. "Having a visionary founder is great, but the founder needs to have someone who writes good code, and they must be standing right next to you."

Pulver is too impatient for PowerPoints or videos. "I'm here," he says. "Talk to me. Don't try to impress me with names of people who already made the commitment to invest in you. I don't care about who's on your advisory board." And when he says "no," he means no, not yes with a lower valuation.

OUTSIDE EYES AND EARS

Perhaps the biggest benefit an experienced angel investor can offer a founder is a set of outside eyes and ears. Living the startup life is a submerging experience for most founders. You live and breathe the startup 24/7. It's often difficult for founders to find their bearings under such conditions. Usually everyone involved in the startup is literally breathing the same air, sharing the same assumptions, working with the same metrics, and occasionally drinking the same Kool-Aid. Having an experienced angel who is willing to talk to you, challenge your assumptions, and ask pointed questions is priceless.

Here are five ongoing advantages that angels earned by successful investor raising can deliver to your startup:

- **A guide who's been there.** It's not easy to be the founder of a company. Someone has to make the decisions, and that's true even in the most cohesive of teams. Teams don't make decisions; some individual has to take the responsibility, and that individual is you. Leaders quickly learn that executive responsibility is an inherently isolating task. As soon as a CEO accepts leadership, relationships with former peers suddenly begin to shift in ways that leave leaders feeling alone, like no one understands them. This perception is based on reality. Just ask anyone who has embraced leadership, from the school teacher who is named principal to the founder who is now CEO. What was equal suddenly is not. Jealousies and undermining behaviors can ensue. Most leaders report that the most challenging aspect of leadership is that it gets lonely at the top. It's a reality that all startups confront.

- **Access to the truth.** Getting authentic information when you are at the top is also a challenge. There is something in human beings that resists honesty with leaders, especially when things are not going well. Maybe it's all those fears of the leader killing the messenger. One CEO told me, "The last day I knew I was funny was the day I was appointed CEO."

- **Recruiting.** Hopefully, the time will come when your startup needs to staff up. Angels can be very helpful in recruiting because we meet lots of smart, talented people every day. Startups often under-utilize the angels they have raised when it comes to recruiting. For example, comiXology, the digital comic book startup I introduced in Chapter 4, was recruiting for a chief marketing officer (CMO). This is a critical position, so founder David Steinberger asked me to interview two of the executives who had survived a series of internal interviews. He liked both candidates and seemed willing to offer a position to either one. I think he was surprised and a bit frustrated when I recommended that he keep looking. For the next set of candidates, I asked David and his team to sit in on my interviews so they could see my interviewing techniques and the way I evaluate candidates. I think they came to understand and respect the power of my interviewing approach to reveal the strengths and weaknesses of candidates. I know their organization and what kind of individual will succeed in that culture. They trusted me to save them the headache and expense of a bad hire.

- **Raising additional equity.** Let me be blunt. When it comes time for you to raise additional rounds, you want to be confident that your original angel will be there for you not only to participate but to champion you to other investors.

- **Building relationships.** If there is one thing that angels need to be good at, it is helping the startups we invest in to build relationships. We do so by being a resource for introductions of all kinds: potential partners, experts such as lawyers and accountants, customers, potential recruits, and sources of capital.

All this is by way of saying that a smart-money investor on your team can be an invaluable resource to think out loud with you as you make the thousands of decisions necessary to grow your business. If you pick wisely, a smart-money investor can be called on for mentoring by serving, formally or informally, on a board of advisors, and in other capacities, structured and unstructured. A thoughtful smart-money investor is in the best position to encourage a founder to work "on" the business instead of "in" the business.

CHAPTER 7 TAKEAWAYS

- Investor raising is about creating relationships.

- It's not the money that really helps you but a long-term relationship with a smart angel.

- It's not easy to turn down money, but doing so may make sense.

- An important question to ask of angels: Do you write checks?

- Angels raised by successful investor raising generate ongoing benefits.

Don't Hurt the Ones Who Love You

For most startups, the first source of funding is the people closest to the entrepreneur. This makes perfect sense. It's easiest to approach the people who know you best and want to believe in you the most.

After all, trust has been established. They know you and often know your work ethic. They want to be helpful. In many cases, such investments are more like gifts than true debt that has to be repaid. In terms of startup financing, friends and family (F&F) money is low-hanging fruit, but be careful about accepting it in a less than professional way.

When I consider your opportunity, I fully expect that you will have F&F investors. According to the Global Entrepreneurship Monitor (Babson College and the London Business School), friends and family investing annually accounts for $50 to $75 billion in early stage capital in the United States. This is two to three times the amount of money invested annually by either angel investors or venture capitalists.

I always encourage entrepreneurs to consider all potential levels of financing, from the very beginning through to the exit. I want you to actually map out the funding process. Think of it as a series of steps. At each step consider how much funding you need and over what period of time you're going to need the investment. It's actually quite a logical process. The only problem is, entrepreneurs rarely treat this first investment with rigor, thoughtful professionalism and legal discipline.

Unfortunately, what happens is that F&F, the people who deserve the best outcomes, don't get the benefit they deserve and in many cases get financially hurt. I get very upset when I see this, because these are the people who take the biggest risks and should receive the best returns.

For entrepreneurs, F&F money represents the smallest increments of funding yet claims the most time to manage. Annette McLellan, an entrepreneur in the biomedical field in Park City, Utah, knows this firsthand. She raised $400,000 for her medical devices company entirely from F&F and came away with two lessons. First, it's a lot more work managing this class of investment. "It's all about the fact that F&F investors have ongoing relationships with me, and they believe they can and should be able to talk to me about their investment," says McLellan. With 45 investors in the F&F pool, that's a lot of ongoing conversations.

The second lesson was how little power she had to protect the position of those early investors. "The reality is that new money sees little value in old money, particularly from the F&F folks," she says. McLellan protected her F&F investors by issuing convertible notes with appropriately high valuation discounts to the next round of financing. The effect of doing so allowed McClellan's F&F investors to reap the benefits of the upside of a VC valuation.

It's usually a misnomer to say that friends and family have invested in your business. It's almost always the case that they have invested in you. After all, they are impressed by your loyalty, integrity, proven smarts, demonstrated work ethic, curiosity, intelligence, and all around excellence. They are willing to invest in you because they care. This reality creates the potential for a number of problems, and entrepreneurs need to be aware of the risks. In too many cases, it's not clear whether the money is a gift or a loan. One of the chief risks is that emotions may get in the way of what is, after all, a highly speculative business transaction.

When F&F investments are structured well, everyone wins. If you make your numbers and you go for an angel or later VC round, everyone can be happy. But unfortunately too many entrepreneurs don't think the process through and unintentionally hurt the ones who love them most.

The issue is that although F&F money is real money, too many entrepreneurs tend to think of it as money that doesn't have to repaid. To be fair, many uncles and brothers-in-law and former college roommates provide funding without clear agreements. Is the money a loan? A gift? The paperwork governing the terms of repayment somehow never gets completed. I've heard some founders say, "My aunt will sign anything I put in front of her." I've seen too many cases where family is mistreated.

You'd think that this would be a huge problem, with stories of millions of conflicts between F&F investors and the founders they supported. In fact, such stories are not hard to find. But the reality is that these kinds of squabbles are actually less common than you might think. That's because so few startups succeed. In other words, the potential for squabbling arises only when a startup is acquired or exits through an IPO and there are considerable sums to be doled out to investors. When there's nothing left to fight about, the lack of agreements rarely becomes an issue.

MANAGE EXPECTATIONS

I believe that it's your responsibility, as a founder, to treat the ones who love you professionally. It's better for everyone to treat it as a business relationship. The failure to treat these investments with the same precision you treat angel or VC money will not only ruin family Thanksgivings for years to come, but it will complicate and even derail subsequent rounds. To manage your investor's expectations, you have to start by managing your own. You start by being principled.

One important way to keep the F&F investing process professional is to hire the best lawyer you can afford. This is definitely not a role for your brother-in-law. First, an experienced startup lawyer can help you understand the different options that you have for raising money. Most startups find it impossible to get a bank to approve a business loan for the startup which, after all, can't offer the bank any collateral. Out of desperation, some entrepreneurs take out a personal loan to invest in the startup. I don't recommend this course, because you will have to repay the loan even if the startup fails. That's why getting money from F&F becomes so tempting.

There are strict laws regulating investments in risky ventures (and there are few ventures more risky than a startup). These rules govern who may or may not invest and what information you need to give them before they invest. A lawyer is helpful every step of the way.

As an angel investor, I expect to see some F&F friends and family participation when I am considering an investment. Linda Holliday puts it this way: "If you come from a privileged background where an angel assumes there's such money available, you better have some." But she is quick to add that if you come from a humble background, no angel will judge you for not having F&F investments.

Most founders don't realize that raising money is an ongoing process, that they will need successive rounds of capital raising as the startup evolves. I like to see startups get smart about raising money as early as possible, not just as a singular event but as an ongoing part of the evolution and development of their business. If they do, it'll make the angel rounds much easier.

Just recently, I met with a group of founders who had a brilliant concept for a startup. I was very impressed and prepared to invest. I wasn't surprised that that group had secured a fair amount of F&F money. Anyone could see their concept was very exciting. Trouble is, the group had no clear sense of the value of the company and the value of the shares they were giving away.

So when it came to the angel round, I had to confront the team with a painful fact: they had given away too much of the company too soon. I had them take a hard look at the capitalization table, a summary of who owns how much of their company at this point in time. The bottom line was that they had given so much equity away that after I took my share, there would be too little equity left to keep the founder properly incentivized, a situation no investor ever wants to see. Even if the founders were willing to move forward with so little equity, it's simply not workable in the long run. There will likely be another round with further dilution.

The solution in this case is not pretty. The founders had to go back to the friends and family who first invested in them and say, "Oops, we have a problem. We can't raise money because we were too generous with you—we gave away too much of the company for too little, so now we need to ask that you reduce your ownership of the company."

No one likes to hear this. Luckily in this instance, the team made a good case, and the friends and family returned some of the equity so the founders wouldn't be so diluted they would no longer have skin in the game. So as painful as those conversations must have been, the situation worked out for this startup. But all this trauma could have been avoided had the founders thought strategically about the various investment steps they would require as they evolved. I realize it's difficult to look at the big picture when you're not even a company, but that's what successful entrepreneurs have to do.

What the founders in this case reluctantly did was to "cram down" their friends and family. As someone who has been on the receiving end of actions that dilute my ownership of a company, I can tell you it's no fun. And I want to be clear: I think friends and family deserve a good chance of having their gamble on a startup pay off handsomely. They, after all, were the first to believe in the founders, and they took the most risk. I think the people who take the most risk should get the most reward. But the valuations have to be well thought out, or everyone loses.

Accepting money from F&F can be fraught with difficulties. My own take on accepting F&F money is based less on the sophistication of the entrepreneur than on the sophistication of the individual approached to invest in an F&F round. Here's the test: is the F&F member savvy about business practices? Does she have significant investments in the bond or equities markets? Is she an active trader? Has she established a track record of investing in family opportunities, and has she developed formal practices for documenting those investments? Is she advised by a neutral lawyer, accountant, or tax adviser?

There are no guarantees, but if you're dealing with someone sophisticated in financial matters and who is well-advised, then I think accepting F&F money is warranted. If in doubt, seek money elsewhere. It will be more expensive in the short run, but trust me, you can't afford cheap money that puts dear relationships at risk.

FRIENDS AND FAMILY
INVESTING CHECKLIST

Mistakes in the F&F round can really complicate matters for startups. Here are five practices to minimize the risks.

1. **Make sure the money is discretionary.** In other words, don't take money from friends and family if you don't think they can afford to lose it—even if they say they are willing to take the risk. If you're not sure on this matter, then don't take their money.

2. **Be professional about it.** Treat the transaction as professionally as you would expect to be treated by an

angel investor or VC. Treat it as an arms-length transaction. As a start, strongly encourage the F&F to be represented by an objective adviser. Is it a loan? Make sure everyone understands the terms, and have a lawyer prepare a promissory note for the friend or family member. A promissory note is like an IOU but a lot more costly to prepare. And while the F&F member may suggest a very low interest rate, insist on paying market rates for commercial loans. The IRS usually treats investments with below-market interest rates as gifts, instigating some nasty tax consequences for both the lender and the recipient.

3. **Tie payments to your cash flow.** In other words, try to avoid obligations with fixed repayment schedules. Consider instead "cash flow" obligations, in which your investors will receive a percentage of your operating cash flow (if any) until they either have been repaid in full with interest or have achieved a specified percentage return on their investment.

4. **Loans are easier than equity.** I generally think that offering debt is better than offering equity. When you offer F&F members equity, they are legally your business partners. Do you really want Uncle Freddy as a business partner? It's better to treat such investments as loans. But if your F&F members insist on equity, try to make it nonvoting stock, so they can't insist on being consulted on every management decision.

5. **Pay the money back, with thanks, as quickly as you can.** Some company founders tell me that borrowing money from friends or family inspires them to work even harder, so as not to disappoint their investors. Tim Westergren persisted with his startup, Pandora Radio, long after other founders would have turned the dial, in large part because he didn't want to lose the money invested by his family. "I've brought everyone into it and can't turn back," Westergren says.

By the same token, the last thing Scott Cook, the founder-CEO of personal-finance software company Intuit, wanted to do was take money from family. But 25 failed pitches later, a desperate Cook caved in and borrowed from his parents' retirement savings. "What kept me going was just fear that I didn't know how I'd ever pay back the money," Cook recalls.

CHAPTER 8 TAKEAWAYS

- Friends and family don't invest in the startup; they invest in you.

- Angels expect most investments to include some F&F participation.

- Protect F&F by having formal agreements and well-considered valuations.

- Manage expectations of F&F.

Going Belly to Belly with Your Customer

9

What entrepreneurs impress me most? The ones who have the courage and have taken the effort to seek out and actually talk to prospects and customers and other stakeholders. That's what I call going belly to belly with customers.

What's the best way to determine what customers want? Watch them. I remember one student who had an idea for a business in the wedding planning space. I had my doubts about the business model—was there anything really new about it?—but I was totally impressed by the research this student did.

It wasn't easy for this shy student, but he went to Kleinfeld Bridal in New York City, ground zero for bridal parties preparing for expensive weddings. He respectfully approached women—it was all women—entering and exiting the store to ask them if they would participate in a short survey. He gained important insights from the information he gathered.

At one point, a cranky man came out of Kleinfeld's to challenge the student about accosting the store's customers. The student explained his purpose. The man smiled and introduced himself as the general manager of Kleinfeld's. He said he was interested in hearing more and invited the student inside the store to talk. They talked for two hours. In addition to gaining very valuable and actionable information, the student gained an

125

important ally. The general manager agreed to be on the student's advisory committee. This level of customer engagement is major evidence that the entrepreneur is ready to do the heavy lifting required to launch a business. This student is the kind of entrepreneur I want to back.

Sadly, I have too many conversations with startups that begin like this:

Me: How many customers have you actually spoken to?

Startup: A handful.

I'm already skeptical. I'm asking for an important number that startups should be proud of trumpeting. I believe that startups should move heaven and earth to live and breathe the air of customers. That's the only way startups can parse out the problems that customers actually have and discern how the startup's product can be a solution for those problems. The conversation generally goes downhill from here:

Me: Okay, so what do you want a prospective customer to do?

Startup: Go to our website. They will find the solution they need.

Me: The solution is just hanging there?

Startup: Well, first they have to register.

Me: Oh, they have to register? Then what happens?

Startup: Then they make a small payment.

Me: How small? And have you done any research to determine the percentage of customers who are willing to provide their information, register, and pay?

I don't enjoy giving startups the third degree like this, but they need to think out the whole process a lot better if they want to get me to invest. The main problem is that most startups don't really understand the relationship they are hoping to build with customers. They haven't thought through how their product will integrate into the life, behaviors, and day to day operations of their customers. Sometimes it's as simple as failing to understand and use the customer's vernacular. So they spin their wheels selling features that don't matter to customers.

Much of this confusion comes from startups failing to have a high-resolution image of their customers. The most promising startups have done research into the demographics of their typical customers: age, gender, geography, lifestyle, income, aspiration, brand preferences, shopping habits. They learn which words and phrases resonate with their customers. This research doesn't come cheap or easy, but it's available with a little work.

A good place to actually watch customers is at trade shows, events which aggregate a large number of potential customers in one location. I admire startups that have arranged to have a presence at trade shows to get belly to belly with customers. The idea is not to convert attendees to paying users but rather to let you observe them playing with your product. Beta users will say any number of things about how great your product is, but the value of a hundred conversations is not equal to one instance of seeing a prospect actually use your product. That's what tells you which features are actually needed.

WHAT SOLUTION IS THE CUSTOMER HIRING?

A good way to consider the marketability of a product or service is to ask this question: What exactly is the customer hiring when he or she buys my product or service?

Framing the question this way is much more powerful than the traditional problem-solution way of looking at products. The manufacturer of a three-eighths-inch drill bit is looking not for a customer who requires a three-eighths-inch drill bit but rather a customer who requires a three-eighths-inch hole. By this reasoning, the job the customer is hiring the product to do is to create a hole of a specific diameter.

This question has immediate real-world implications for every startup, but answering the question requires going belly to belly with customers. In his Harvard MBA course, Professor Clayton Christensen, author of *The Innovator's Dilemma,* tells a story about how his consulting company helped a restaurant chain increase milkshake sales.

Christensen began by segmenting the market by both product (milkshakes) and by demographic relevance (age, gender, income, time of purchase, to-go or consumed in restaurant, etc.). Then his company conducted a number of focus groups to identify the characteristics that customers demanded of milkshakes (packaging, color, smoothness, chunkiness, thickness, thinness, etc.). Based on feedback from the focus groups, the company went back to the kitchen and adjusted the consistency, flavor, and presentation of its milkshakes. But despite all this, milkshake sales remained flat.

Christensen then decided to switch logical frameworks. Instead of focusing on what customers said they wanted, he decided to concentrate on how customers actually behaved. The professor dispatched a team of observers to sit in restaurants and document everything they could about the customers actually buying milkshakes. An immediate surprise surfaced: many of the milkshakes were purchased early in the morning by people who ordered them to go and then got in their cars and drove away. Moreover, many of them were repeat customers.

After some days of observation, the researchers approached these customers to get more information about why they were buying milkshakes. In doing so, the researchers looked to determine the "job" that customers were "hiring" milkshakes to do.

"Most of the customers, it turned out, bought [the milkshake] to do a similar job," writes Christensen in "Integrating Around the Job to Be Done," a teaching note published by the Harvard Business School:

> They faced a long, boring commute and needed something
> to keep that extra hand busy and to make the commute
> more interesting. They weren't yet hungry, but knew
> that they'd be hungry by 10 a.m.; they wanted to have
> something tasty to stave off hunger. And the commuters
> faced constraints: They were in a hurry, they were
> wearing business clothes, and they had (at most) one
> free hand.

Thanks to the work of Christensen's team, the client company finally understood what customers were hiring the milkshakes to do. The restaurant responded by creating a morning milkshake that was noticeably thicker (to last through a long commute) and more complex (with chunks of fruit or nuts). Milkshake sales took off. That's going belly to belly with your customer by observing how they behave with your product.

MARKET

The reliable knowledge of a market is one obligatory success factor for a startup. Moreover, the market must be locatable (you must know where it is and how to find it at a predictable cost) and substantial. It won't do to pin your success on a market that is either so diffuse that you can't pin it down or so small as to make its location irrelevant. No startup succeeds unless it meets the real needs of a real group of people.

A market is different than a category. When Federal Express (now FedEx) began, it was criticized because the market for overnight delivery was new. But just because it was new didn't mean it wasn't locatable and substantial. Even smart people err by mistaking category for market.

I initially want to focus on how well you know your customers and their behaviors and why you believe you have a better way for them to work or play. I'm particularly interested in how you translate customer insights into engagement capabilities with thoughtful features that add value to their experience. But even if I know everything about the baseline needs of your customer, I can predict only 50 percent of your long-term prospects for success.

IQ IS OVERRATED

Research shows that only about 25 percent of success is predicted by IQ. That's because most of whatever long-term success you attain is predicted not by your intelligence—or by the external circumstances of your customers, the economy, or your competitors—but by the way you and your partners process the world. Seventy-five percent of success is predicted by your optimism level, your social support, and (perhaps most of all for entrepreneurs) your ability to see stress as a challenge instead of as a threat, according to Shawn Achor in a fabulous TED talk called "The Happy Secret to Better Work."

TED is a nonprofit that since 1984 has aggregated thousands of the most delectable presentations around its broad themes of technology, entertainment, and design. The two annual TED conferences, in Long Beach/Palm Springs and Edinburgh, Scotland, bring together the world's most fascinating thinkers and doers, who are challenged to give the talks of their lives (in 18 minutes or less).

If you think your presentation is as good as it gets, watch a few TED videos and weep. Most are so good they will make you want to throw away everything you have and start anew. It might not be a bad idea. Almost every TED talk on the website is a model of pristine presentationship.

Most entrepreneurs are driven, Type-A individuals, just like me and many other early-stage investors. We remain in the game because we love the thrill of the startup, even if we don't quite have the energy required to run a startup. Investing allows us to enjoy the thrills without having to do all the heavy lifting. My point is that I spend a lot of time with success-seeking, Type-A entrepreneurs, and I've noticed something alarming.

Why can't entrepreneurs be satisfied with success? I certainly haven't met any who can, including me. Once we achieve some goal we set for ourselves, we tend to redefine the goal. We move the goalposts. We have a good paying job, we want a better paying job; we started a company, we have to start a more successful company; we hit our sales quota, we raise our quota. The problem is, when are we ever satisfied?

CHAPTER 9 TAKEAWAYS

- Going belly to belly with customers means knowing everything about a customer from firsthand experience.

- Determine what customers are hiring when they use your product or service.

- Have a reliable idea of the size of the market.

- IQ is overrated.

Due Diligence
and Do Diligence

Several months ago I met with a group of younger angel investors, and I explained how I try to confirm some of the things in the pitches I hear. They looked at me with amazement and said, "Oh, you're one of the old-style angels."

Frankly, I couldn't believe my ears. "What do you mean?"

"Oh, we roll in a new way," they said. "We think due diligence is a waste of time. We're good judges of these things. If we like the idea and like the team, we give them money."

Since then I've met many angels who share this point of view. Why bother verifying a lot of stuff on résumés or who owns what intellectual property, when the real issue is the idea and the intelligence of the team, details that can be validated just by talking to people? It's also true that due diligence takes time. On average, angel investors spend seven hours on due diligence per investment. That can seem burdensome, especially if an investor wants a diverse portfolio.

But I think if you're going to be an angel, then you should invest the time and energy to do it well. The research is absolutely clear on this: there is a direct link between investment returns and the length of time you spend on due diligence. According to a 2007 study for the Angel Resource Institute, "Returns of Angels in Groups," Robert Wiltbank of Willamette

University found that angel investors who devoted less than 20 hours of due diligence per opportunity received portfolio returns of ×1.1 as compared with the ×7.1 returns by those who spent more than 40 hours on due diligence. It's clear there's a positive correlation between the time spent on due diligence and portfolio returns.

CALL IT DISCOVERY

I know that many founders dread this step. Frankly, the words "due diligence" frighten a lot of entrepreneurs. I find the term "discovery" less threatening.

By any term, the concept is very simple. It's an investigation or audit of a potential investment. It is completed before a startup receives an infusion of equity capital from the investor. The goal of the process is to give investors an objective look at weaknesses, potential liabilities, and other exposures so they can better assess the risks of the investment. Due diligence is all about mitigating risk.

There's risk in every investment; no startup is perfect. It's always easy to find a reason for saying no to any opportunity. I've met a lot of angels who put so much effort into due diligence that they hesitate to invest in anything. It's analysis paralysis.

Due diligence becomes a trap if it's applied only to identify reasons *not* to invest in a startup. I believe the process should equally be applied to identify reasons to invest with enthusiasm. I call this process "do" diligence.

Other angels use do diligence to give themselves "permission to believe," a concept I discussed in Chapter 4. Mature angels understand that risk can't be eliminated. Due diligence can go a long way toward mitigating avoidable risks. And do diligence underscores the fact that every startup offers bright, shiny opportunities for profit. It's a question of balance.

EAST AND WEST

In the United States, regional differences in due diligence further complicate matters. No one should be surprised to learn that the conversation I recounted at the beginning of this chapter occurred in California. Silicon Valley angels are more laid back about everything, including due diligence.

The kind of due diligence an angel engages in reflects his or her experience. On the East Coast, angels tends to come out of the finance world, and they often want to do what I call "spreadsheet due diligence."

The proponents of relaxed or no due diligence believe that the numbers underlying the presentations are fantasies anyway. Due diligence consumes a lot of time for what is often, from the angel's perspective, a small investment. In such cases, it's more meaningful to have a conversation with the team about how they intend to go to market.

Adam Dinow, a partner in the New York law office of Wilson Sonsini Goodrich & Rosati, is deeply involved in the New York technology community. He serves on the board of directors of NY Tech Meetup, the nonprofit organization at the heart of the New York Angels tech community, with over 30,000 members. Adam represents businesses at all stages of their life cycle, from incorporation to exit, with an emphasis on working with entrepreneurs and fast-paced, rapid-growth enterprises. You'd figure he has a clear opinion of due diligence, and he does.

"The numbers mean nothing; legal due diligence means nothing," Dinow says. "I've worked with investors who go through excruciating due diligence and those who write checks on a whim. The most critical piece is to get comfortable with the entrepreneur and their values, to know he or she is sharp enough to know when something isn't working."

Dinow's main point is that the investing world is moving too fast for due diligence overkill. "When a company can't bring in

$400,000 on an angel round because the due diligence takes too long, that's a problem. In this game, angels are either doing it or not; they can't stretch these companies out for too long," he says.

Some angels ignore due diligence and then try to protect their investments with indemnifications and warranties. Basically, angel investors and startups make representations and warranties to one other in the acquisition agreement. The startup's representations and warranties provide a mechanism for the angel to walk away from or possibly to renegotiate the terms of the investment if, between signing the term sheet and closing the deal, the angel discovers facts that are contrary to the representations and warranties.

"I don't believe an angel investor can legislate due diligence," says Dinow. "Indemnifications and warranties cannot be a substitute for determining up front who you do business with."

Alain Bankier, introduced in Chapter 5, got his start as an investment banker and applies his quantitative skills to every opportunity, so you'd expect him to incline toward the rigorous end of the due diligence spectrum.

"I am very far from the guy who meets a smart entrepreneur and immediately whips out my checkbook," Bankier says. "On the other hand, I am not a due-diligence-to-death guy, either. The research is pretty convincing that angels dramatically increase their chances of return when they apply some measure of due diligence."

One problem is how to do meaningful due diligence on pre-revenue startups. Bankier has evolved a process that looks more like competitive analysis. He wants to have decent confidence that Microsoft, as far as one can tell from available information, is not going to roll out something similar to the product of the startup he's considering. Or even worse, there's already a better mousetrap out there in beta. He also scrutinizes the startup's market projections, to see if they are realistic.

For example, if a startup in a multibillion dollar market indicates it intends to have $20 million of the market in year four, that's a red flag. "Why are they shooting so low?" Bankier wonders. The reverse is also true. "It makes me nervous to see a startup claim $100 million share in a $1 billion market," he says. "Really? You expect to grab 10 percent?"

We are now seeing angels outsourcing due diligence to entities they assume will do it better. In one case, the entity is Y Combinator, the elite accelerator. Yuri Milner's DST Fund and Ron Conway's SV Angel fund recently announced that they will invest in every single startup coming out of Y Combinator. The seed rounds will provide $150,000 to every single one of the 40 startups that wants it, without any due diligence on their own part whatsoever. The capital is in the form of convertible debt with no cap and no discount. The loan will convert when and if the startup raises a proper angel or VC capital round at the same valuation that's set in the round. Most convertible debt has a valuation ceiling and also gets a discount on conversion. The angels are banking on the premise that Y Combinator, in vetting the startups it stewards, has performed satisfactory due diligence.

Milner has effectively shut out any other angel investors by offering such attractive terms. It's almost free money. I'd be surprised if any of the 40 startups in each Y Combinator class decline such an offer.

ANTICIPATE DUE DILIGENCE

Knowing that it's coming, why not anticipate due diligence questions and address them *before* the angel asks? I promise you, angels will be impressed.

It takes a lot of time to prepare for these questions properly. But you'll actually save time over the long term, because you will be asked for this information often. Most investors will want details about your team, stock ownership, other investors, IP, etc.

If you have this information available, don't wait until you are asked for it.

David S. Rose, the CEO of Gust and founder of New York Angels, has raised over $50 million from venture capitalists for companies that he has founded. His approach to due diligence is proactive: before he even meets with an investor, he has already taken a complete list of items that VCs often request during due diligence and compiled them all into one big binder. That way, when a potential investor starts asking about the details, David can simply hand him or her the binder, and say "here you go!"

And if there's some negative information that's going to come out anyway, volunteer it. For example, if there is a dispute about your IP, don't wait for the angel to find it. If you volunteer the information, you project confidence, and you and the angel have an opportunity to discuss the issue. Such conversations are much less agreeable if the angel learns about the problem elsewhere first.

Don't be one of those startups that screws up the due diligence step. It's not enough to assume that the business plan documents and financials speak for themselves. Yes, the business plan and all supporting documents must be up to the minute, synchronized, and in the hands of every founder. And the entire team must be on the same page. Every founder must know the startup's strengths and especially its weaknesses (because that's where angel attention will be focused) and practice responding to potential objections.

It's not just the investor auditing the founder; the founder gets to audit the investor. Far from being insulted by having questions turned on me, I welcome it. I expect it. I'm actually disappointed when a startup fails to do its due diligence on me. I'm not the right investor for every opportunity. I want the entrepreneurs who approach me for funding to be absolutely clear that they want *me* as an investing partner. I like to see a certain peer relationship between the investor and the entrepreneur. A reciprocal due diligence dance keeps the partnership in balance.

Most investors welcome a reasonable level of due diligence from entrepreneurs. If an investor resists, that's a bad sign. I suggest the founder look elsewhere.

Jay Turo, CEO of GroupThink and an angel investor, uses social media to conduct due diligence on entrepreneurs. "You're naked out there," Turo says. The good news is that entrepreneurs can turn the same social media tools on angels. Appendix C describes five indispensable tools for entrepreneurs to use as they conduct due diligence on angel investors: LinkedIn, Gust, AngelList, TechCrunch, and Quora.

COMMON DUE DILIGENCE ISSUES

Early-stage equity investors approach due diligence in different ways, but here are a handful of common issues on which entrepreneurs should always expect to be scrutinized:

* **The team.** Convene the team to discuss due diligence. This is a perfect time for the CEO to present the final investor charts and answer any questions. Everyone on the team needs to know what his or her role is for the due diligence. Every team member will likely be separately interviewed. Investors want to determine the commitment, talent, strengths and weaknesses, and management style of each team member. For many investors, the "chemistry" of the team is the number one issue, because we know that a first-rate team with a second-rate idea will always outperform a second-rate team with a first-rate idea. Make sure all résumés are up to date. Give listed references a heads up that the startup is being scrutinized. If due diligence uncovers signs of a team member who doesn't carry his or her own weight, a naysayer, or a dysfunctional team, most investors will back off.

- **Validation of product.** I'm interested in your technology, the current state of your product's development, and customer satisfaction. How ready for market is the product or service? The answer to this question comes from a process called "technical due diligence." Before I invest, I generally spend a day or more with the individuals responsible for engineering, development, and product marketing. I want to evaluate the quality of the startup's development processes as well as the products themselves. Is what you have to offer something consumers need or simply want? Does it work? Is it ready to ship? Are there any issues or certifications that need to be resolved? If the product is in customer hands, I'll ask for a list of customers. I need to have confidence that the product is ready for release and actually has all the features detailed in the presentation.

- **Customers.** Now would be a good time for you to contact key customers and vendors. Explain that they may be called, and use the opportunity to gauge their satisfaction with your company and your product. If there's a problem you can't fix, tell me yourself. You don't want me to be surprised. Customers are key to success. I can be a pretty good resource for a startup, but I can't make customers buy anything, and without actual customers eventually parting with their money in exchange for a good or service, there is no business. So I will ask for lists of potential customers to call. I'll start with your (undoubtedly well-rehearsed) reference list but will quickly try to get them off-script and go from there. I will also try to ascertain the sustainability of the market. Does the startup enjoy key differentiators or significant barriers to entry? If not, even the best markets can be poached by new competitors.

- **Size of the market.** A great product or service is critical, but it's not enough. One of the criteria for a good investment is a large and fast-growing market. I'll determine the actual size of the potential market and the market share you can reasonably expect to capture. I'll examine the sales and marketing strategy you expect to deliver that market share. This will involve an analysis of your distribution channels, promotion, and pricing strategy. I need to get an independent reading on barriers to entry, competition, and price sensitivity.

- **Intellectual property.** I need to be confident that the startup's claims to its intellectual property (patents, trademarks, copyrights, etc.) are legally sound. For many startups, the intellectual property is the sole basis for the valuation of the company, so investors need to be confident that it's real.

- **Business integrity.** Every entrepreneur, every startup, leaves a trail of business transactions in its wake. As much as I am able, I like to trace that trail backward to determine how well the team has met its previous financial and business milestones. Does the record show evidence of meeting commitments and obligations? Or is the trail peppered with unpaid bills, disgruntled landlords, active lawsuits, or bankruptcies? Any one of these is generally a deal breaker for me.

DREADING DUE DILIGENCE

Why should due diligence be so threatening? If I were a founder, I'd be suspicious of an investor who is willing to write me a check on the basis of a single pitch. I'd expect the investor to conduct an objective check of my business model, talk to a few of my customers, and verify that the product or service, team background, and revenue projections are as represented. If the results do not match the representations, a conversation needs to follow.

I speak from experience. There is no substitute for due diligence, as I think the new generation of angels will discover to their dismay. I've been burned many times by making bets solely on the basis of my initial judgment, only to find out later that my investment was squandered by founders without integrity. There's really only one way to determine an individual's integrity: to consider how that person acts—or has acted—when he or she thinks no one is looking. That's what due diligence does. In a disciplined way, it looks at an individual's achievements and behavior, both good and bad.

I personally pay more attention to some things than others. Integrity is of paramount importance to me. I want to confirm that the educational credentials on the résumé are as represented. I also think the way an individual handles money is hugely revealing. I want to see if the founder has handled debt with integrity or if he has left a trail of landlords, merchants, financial institutions, and other investors holding the bag. In the stock market, we are reminded that past results do not guarantee future performance. But when it comes to character, past behavior is the most reliable predictor of future performance.

CHAPTER 10 TAKEAWAYS

- Due diligence gathers evidence for not investing.

- Do diligence gathers evidence for investing with enthusiasm.

- Anticipate due diligence.

- Founders need to do due diligence on angels.

Accelerators, Incubators, and Crowdfunding

11

Entrepreneurs seeking early-stage funding now can exploit three exciting new developments: accelerators, incubators, and crowdfunding.

Accelerators and incubators have become an increasingly dynamic part of the tech startup/angel investing ecosystem in recent years. Both programs provide startups with mentorship, advice, practical training, and contacts to guide them from idea to product development to product launch. A number of hot startups have emerged from these programs, encouraging angel investors to take a good look at the startups graduating from the best programs.

Crowdfunding, in which large numbers of ordinary people invest small amounts online to fund early startups, is destined to supplement the traditional angel and perhaps even VC funding process. Some industry watchers predict that crowdfunding will replace angels. I don't think that's likely, and I'll tell you why, but the phenomenon is real, important, and once it arrives, will be here to stay.

In this chapter, I examine these three developments and the implications for entrepreneurs seeking early-stage funding from angels.

ACCELERATORS AND INCUBATORS

Timing is the key difference between accelerators and incubators.

Accelerators and incubators have similar goals, but they're quite different in their approaches to stewarding startups to success. Both create platforms for entrepreneurs to develop, acquire mentoring, perfect their business presentations, and network among potential investors. Each provides office space and other physical resources. Both can be fantastic learning environments. Both accelerators and incubators are great for transferring knowledge and experience quickly.

In general, an incubator makes startups pay rent to use its facilities, so they are encouraged to stick around as long as possible. In the end, an incubator represents a safe place to grow and work, providing office space and often some marketing support or backroom services. There's usually no one pressuring you to move faster.

Accelerators are all about kicking startups out of the nest after three to four months to see if they'll fly. I'm sensitive to the fact that these companies are often not supported after they leave. I'd like to see accelerators develop some kind of graduate program for companies that need continued guidance and support.

DOING MORE SMARTER, FASTER

The idea behind accelerators is to do more smarter and faster. "Accelerators don't feel very protective or nurturing," says Dan Kador, CTO of Keen IO , who went through the TechStars Cloud accelerator. "TechStars throws entrepreneurs together with a mix of mentors and potential investors and leaves it to the entrepreneurs to figure out how to best take advantage of that opportunity. It's sink or swim."

Another difference between accelerators and incubators is that incubators charge rent whereas accelerators acquire a stake in the startup. An accelerator generally takes 6 to 8 percent of a startup's equity in return for a three-month program offering mentorship, startup services, legal support, and overhead.

Startups that graduate from accelerators often attract investment capital because accelerators are perceived to mitigate the risk for angel investors, and founders have been taught how to raise money and how to create Hollywood-like presentations that culminate in a demo day that draws many angels.

Incubated startups, on the other hand, usually begin with little or no capital, which is one reason incubated companies tend to struggle. Incubators were all the rage during the dot-com buildup of the 1990s, with many of them associated with universities or economic development agencies. What smart incubators do is bring together startups that have much in common, such as all-biotech or all-social-media startups, to optimize the conditions for creating synergies. When the dot-com bubble burst, most incubators folded.

Murat Aktihanoglu is founder and managing director of the New York–based Entrepreneurs Roundtable Accelerator. The accelerator runs sessions funding 10 technology, Internet, and mobile startups and provides free space, free services, and free mentoring with its 120 mentors (among whom I'm proud to count myself), and 10 operational partners and interns. "After our graduates finish our program, we encourage them to find a good incubator for further development," Murat says. "Startups really need to be with other startups. The synergies are amazing. No startup founders want to be in a room on their own."

Not all entrepreneurs need incubators or accelerators. "Facebook's Mark Zuckerberg would have been a terrible fit for an accelerator," says Gabriella Draney, cofounder and managing partner of Tech Wildcatters, a Dallas-based accelerator that boasts a vertical specialization focusing on B2B startups. "Zuckerberg wouldn't have been happy with the program, or more likely, the program wouldn't have been happy with him," Draney says. "Certain people are the type to want to go off on their own. The accelerator mold tends to be more about the community."

Y COMBINATOR AND TECHSTARS

There are dozens of accelerators around the country, but the two most prominent and selective are Y Combinator and TechStars, according to *Forbes* magazine. Both programs are more selective than Harvard. Thousands of startups apply. TechStars, based in Boulder, Colorado, invests its money and time in only 10 or so companies per program location. TechStars offers programs in Boston, Boulder, New York City, Seattle, and San Antonio on a regular schedule. TechStars invests $118,000 in each company selected for the accelerator. The founders get $18,000 in seed funding plus an optional $100,000 convertible debt note. TechStars provides three months of office space, intensive mentorship, advice from investors with deep domain contacts, and—most valuable—the chance to pitch to angel investors and venture capitalists at the end of the program. TechStars takes 6 percent equity in each of the startups it graduates.

One thing I like about TechStars is its transparency. Its public website reveals the fates of all the companies it has funded, citing their current status, funding raised, employee counts, and more. When this book went to press, the TechStars portfolio had 98 active startups, 10 of which have been acquired. (Eighteen companies, or 14 percent, had failed.) The most significant statistic is that the average TechStars company raised over $1 million in outside financing after leaving the accelerator.

Research suggests that accelerators are more successful than incubators at launching companies. Transparency is one of the great virtues of both Y Combinator and TechStars. In an investing world where there is little real information about results, the leading accelerators actually report on their results.

Paul Graham, one of the visionaries behind Y Combinator (YC), recently reported that of the 36 companies funded in the summer 2010 cycle, 34 (94 percent) either raised more money post-YC or didn't need to. That's an extraordinary record, but the real payday comes when a startup actually gets acquired. How does YC fare on that dimension? The jury is still out, because the numbers are still coming in. "The problem with measuring exits is that they take a long time," says Graham, "and the most successful companies tend to take the longest." Even seven years—the number of years YC has been operating—does not provide a sufficient baseline for accurate measurement. Still, YC reports that 25 of the companies it has funded have been acquired, five (8 percent) of them for over $10 million. That's pretty good, but the real value is probably embedded in the startups yet to be acquired.

"From an investor standpoint, accelerators are an efficient way to locate, develop, and test talent that might not be ready for a larger round," says Aktihanoglu, managing founder of the Entrepreneurs Roundtable Accelerator. "From the founder standpoint, they are a great vehicle for bringing exposure, connections, mentorship, and future funding to your company in a hurry."

I totally believe in the value of accelerators. When it comes to funding, they represent the high-end potential of startups, particularly when they have a reputation for quality and a good model for selecting their startups. I try not to miss any demo days. In fact, at an Entrepreneur Roundtable Accelerator demo day in September 2012, I saw more than 20 of my fellow New York Angels in the room. Aktihanoglu was so impressed, he reserved all the front-row seats for the New York Angels. He certainly knows how to make angels feel special.

CROWDFUNDING

Crowdfunding represents the socialization of capital. I'm all for making it easier for startups to acquire capital.

Crowdfunding is an efficient person-to-person way for startups, artists, and activists of all stripes to aggregate small sums from ordinary people anywhere. It is a rapidly emerging phenomenon that combines small online contributions ("micropledges") from many individuals who want to support a project. Crowdfunding circumvents traditional funding mechanisms for early-stage financing such as angel investing, venture capital, and bank loans. Anyone can make online donations with no strings attached or monetary pledges in return for a reward.

Crowdfunding has proven effective for raising seed funding for startups, collecting donations for charity, supplying microcredit in the developing world, and getting donations for political campaigns. Kickstarter and Indiegogo users are pledging funds at a rate of $2 million a week for thousands of projects.

But so far, in the United States at least, there is no meaningful crowdfunding *investing* taking place. The current crowdfunding model is closer to philanthropy than to investing. In the case of the microlender Kiva, lenders get their money back (assuming there is no default) but earn no interest. The only things of value that "funders " in Kickstarter projects usually receive are mention in the credits of a movie, a T-shirt, and sometimes the promise—and occasionally actual delivery—of the product the crowdfunding is intended to develop.

Crowdfunding for startups has historically been complicated by the same securities laws that restrict angel investing to accredited investors. But the Jumpstart Our Business Startups Act that President Obama signed into law in April 2012 promises to drastically change that within the next year. The law, known as the JOBS Act, creates a regulatory framework that lets startups use crowdfunding to raise up to $1 million annually, from investors pledging a total of no more than 10 percent of their annual income or assets across all the investments they make during a year. I'm not holding my breath. When the SEC eventually sets forth rules to implement this law (expected to be late in 2013), the JOBS Act promises to harness "the wisdom of crowds to democratize access to capital for entrepreneurs." But despite the enthusiasm of the entrepreneurial community, and the many crowdfunding platforms that are rushing to be first out of the gate when the new law goes into effect, many experts in the early stage financing world are highly skeptical. "The crowdfunding jewel is fool's gold," according to Daniel Isenberg, professor of management practice at Babson Global and founding executive director of the Babson Entrepreneurship Ecosystem Project. "Crowdfunding equity stock purchases for risky startups—the target of the JOBS Act—cannot work," he says.

I'm all for startups having access to funds. But startups don't just need money. They need mentoring, expertise on how to run a business, and contacts for future growth. That's exactly what "smart money" angels provide. In a crowdsourced model, however, there is no mentoring component because no single investor has enough money at stake in the venture to really take an active interest in its success. Ironically, the lack of mentoring makes the average crowdfunded startup even riskier. This is a real limitation of the crowdfunding model.

The other problem is that when it comes time for formal angel or VC investing, there is real concern about a very large number of investors in the capitalization table. It creates a huge administrative burden. In addition, even if only a small percentage of the crowdsourced investors were to ask for updates or information, it would become a huge time burden for struggling young companies.

The equity part of the crowdfunding process may provide good entertainment, since it's like playing the lottery. And I can see the day when crowdfunding will mature to be an important part of the startup funding ecosystem. But for now, there'll be a lot of individuals getting burned.

Project crowdfunding, however, has already proven to be a great success. Launched in 2009, Kickstarter is a great way to sell things that don't yet exist. David Tisch, the founder of TechStars, says posting a product on Kickstarter allows you to gauge demand. Startups can use evidence of strong Kickstarter demand to support their presentations for more funding from angels and VCs. "For the first time, there's a way to get customer feedback with money attached to it," he said.

The feedback isn't exactly free and provides important clues for startups seeking crowdfunding. While there's no fee for starting a project, if the project is funded, Kickstarter takes 5 percent of contributions. Plus Amazon takes another 3 to 5 percent for processing the payments. If the project is not funded—still the likeliest outcome—there is no charge. Kickstarter, the largest of a number of similar platforms, has raised over $350 million for projects.

The good news with Kickstarter and other crowdfunding sites is that it's possible (albeit rare) for entrepreneurs to raise far more money than they request. Pebble Technology, a three-person startup, sought to raise $100,000 to produce 1,000 wristwatches that can be programmed with different clock faces. "We had tried raising money through the normal routes, and it didn't really work," says Eric Migicovsky, the 25-year-old founder of Pebble. Donors on Kickstarter thought the watches were so cool that Pebble Technology raised $10.3 million before Pebble's self-imposed cap kicked in and ended the crowdfunding.

But beware. Raising money through crowdsourcing is like borrowing money from your closest 10,000 friends and relatives. "It's definitely a lot of pressure," Migicovsky reports. "There are 65,000 people who have preordered a watch that doesn't yet exist." Nearly 9,000 investors feel free to e-mail him, and they do. Migicovsky had to hire someone just to manage his e-mail inbox and post updates. According to Ethan Mollick, a professor of management at the Wharton School of the University of Pennsylvania, 75 percent of design- and technology-related projects on Kickstarter that promise to develop physical products fail to meet their promised deadlines.

It's easy for project creators to be overwhelmed by the success of a crowdfunding campaign. Four college students started Diaspora, a project to build an open alternative to Facebook, with a modest goal of raising $10,000. They actually received $200,000 from 6,500 investors. But three years after starting the project, the founders decided it was too much for them. So they turned the code over to anyone who wanted it. "We wanted to make Diaspora because it was something we believed in, but we got roped into maintaining a relationship with a lot of people," says Max Salzberg, one of the founders. "We weren't prepared to have to deal with that." The team became so consumed with answering e-mails and making T-shirts for contributors that they had little time to build the software. "Going viral was crippling," Salzberg says.

SIX MODELS OF CROWDFUNDING

1. **Good-cause crowdfunding.** This is the most mature variety of crowdfunding. Dozens of online platforms allow people to donate money to projects that are represented as having positive moral and ethical values. Note the word *donate*. There is no investment here in the traditional sense of financial returns, although the intangible value of contributing to something that adds to the world's store of happiness is laudable. StartSomeGood and the Facebook Cause page are examples of this model.

2. **Rewards-based crowdfunding.** Investors send small amounts of money to fund a variety of mostly arts-based or social

change projects. In addition to having the satisfaction of supporting a worthwhile project, investors are promised to immediately receive a pre-determined reward or perk, such as a t-shirt, credits in a movie, or other recognition. No equity or finished product is usually part of the bargain. IndieGoGo is one of the earliest players in this space.

3. **Inventor-based crowdfunding.** This model invites inventors to describe their inventions and request incremental seed money (often spread out over time in line with the inventing cycle). People can make online monetary pledges in return for a reward or as a donation just because they're excited about the project. The major benefit to inventors is that project backers do not expect to be paid back or receive any ownership interest in the project, nor are project owners shackled with onerous state, federal or international regulations in the process. A good example of this model of crowdfunding is Fundageek.

4. **Pre-order crowdfunding.** Under this model, ordinary people make online pledges with their credit cards during a campaign, to pre-order something that does not yet exist. The promise is that the pledges will allow the product to be built for subsequent delivery to the people who funded the development. Sometimes the products are developed; sometimes they are not. That's the risk people accept. This is ecommerce under a different name. There is no concept of investment. Kickstarter is the most well-known player in this space.

5. **Debt-based crowdfunding.** Sometimes called micro-financing or peer-to-peer (P2P) lending, entrepreneurs borrow money from a number of people online and pay them back when and if the project is finished. This has been popular in many developing countries for years via sites like LendingClub and

Kiva. The model is becoming more attractive in the U.S. But there is no real concept of investing in this model in that in the best case only the principal is repaid. No interest is earned.

6. **Equity crowdfunding.** This was established in the United States by the JOBS Act of 2012, and will likely become legal once the SEC publishes the rules for it in late 2013. Equity crowdfunding is the model that most entrepreneurs hope will mature so that individuals can truly invest, in the sense of exchanging risk today for the chance of profit tomorrow. Under this model, large numbers of regular people who are not accredited investors can invest small amounts of money for small amounts of equity in early-stage startups. If it works, this type of crowdfunding may give any number of startups a quick and efficient way to aggregate seed capital. It may substitute or supplement traditional angel funding.

CHAPTER 11 TAKEAWAYS

- The accelerator experience differs from the incubator experience.

- Accelerators encourage startups to work smarter and faster.

- Incubators are about creating a conducive growth environment.

- Crowdfunding can be part of a startup's funding mix, but it can be hard to manage.

- Crowdfunding can complicate a startup's further funding requirements.

It's All About Teammanship

Yes, I know the word doesn't exist, but *teammanship* is an all-encompassing term I use to describe the quality of a startup's team identity and the relationships among its members. When I see teammanship in action, my checkbook comes out.

The right team led by the right leader can do the impossible and create truly breathtaking results. The critical thing is that the people behind the startup have a shared team identity and responsibility. I want teams I invest in to execute on their goals. I tend to invest in startups with a high level of teammanship, even if the initial idea is half-baked. There are no conditions under which I would invest in a startup with low teammanship. Team-building mistakes create bad blood, bad times, and bad products. They pull a team dangerously away from its goals.

Many qualities go into teammanship, but it's mostly about attitudes and shared values in just the right balance. Teammanship means that founders believe the same thing together, that they rationalize and appreciate the value of the startup, and they are pulling as one to meet the customer's needs. The team also recognizes its deficiencies and works hard to plug holes, adding talent where necessary. They represent an orchestration of effort, not a collection of egos trying to outdo one another.

The first element of teammanship is the leader. One of the first questions every angel wants answered is: Who is the leader of the startup? Who is the originator of the idea? Who owns the vision? It's not always the person who gets up and leads the presentation . . . although it should be!

Every angel thinks of teammanship in his or her own way. I know some angels who insist that the leader have a degree from an Ivy League university. I don't put that much stock in academic credentials. Highly educated leaders are good, but I've seen problems on teams where everyone came from places where they were the smartest kids in the school. Egos get in the way, and there's more debate than decision.

I wrote my college thesis on group cohesion, the study of how people work together. When I look at a team, I focus on how well team members work together. How do I do that? I'm not sitting with them as they solve the thousands of day-to-day problems that every startup faces. At presentations, I usually see the CEO and perhaps one or two of the other team members. So that's where I start.

Startups often make a fatal assumption when they attend presentations, business plan competitions, or demo days. They assume they are basically invisible until they take their place on the stage. Big mistake. The truth is, investors are observing you. We learn as much from watching your off-stage behavior as your canned presentation.

Here's a good way to go. Resolve that your formal presentation starts the moment team members leave their homes or offices and ends only when the last team member returns. At all other times, you are "on." Assume the microphones are always on and someone has a camera phone on you at all times. Act like a disciplined team at all times. Watch what you say in the elevator or in the bathroom. You can't believe the damaging stuff I've heard in bathrooms. Wait to debrief until you get back to the privacy of your office.

Always be aware of how you interact with other team members during your presentation. I'm very sensitive to such exchanges, and I pay attention not only to what is said but also to tone of voice and nonverbal cues. If there are team members who aren't at the presentation, I always ask to meet with them too so I can observe the whole team. If I'm interested, I always want to share a few meals with you, as I describe in Chapter 3, "Let's Get to Know Each Other."

INDICATORS THAT REALLY MATTER TO ME

I see some teams making extraordinary efforts to impress me. It pains me when this happens, because the efforts are almost always off the mark. They would be much better off relaxing and focusing their effort on indicators that really matter to me.

Here's a checklist of 10 teammanship indicators that I look for. Most of the questions can be answered by a simple yes or no.

1. Does a team even exist?

2. Do I hear a consistent story?

3. Am I excited about how they work together?

4. Are the founders great leaders?

5. Is the team focused on building a great product?

6. Do they have technical and marketing competence?

7. Is the team fully invested in knowing the financial mechanics of the business?

8. Is the team focused on execution?

9. How strong is the team?

10. Is there a capacity for resolving conflicts?

By the way, these are not questions that I put to the team explicitly. These are the questions I have in the back of my mind as I'm listening. After about half an hour of conversation, I am generally satisfied I have most of the answers I need to make a decision. Founders who understand what unasked questions angel investors have in the backs of their minds will have a great advantage over those who don't, because in their presentations, they can address the critical points.

After listening to the founders, if I'm unsure about one of the 10 items, I assume what I'm looking for is not present. If I get more than one "no," I tend to move on. There's always another team waiting to talk to me.

1. **Does a team even exist?** A group of founders working together does not necessarily mean a team exists. Let me be perfectly clear. A founder with all the equity who has hired a staff, even a world-class staff, does not represent a team. Team members must be peers, even if one member is taking leadership. To me, a team is a group of equals united by a vision who have come together to pursue a common outcome. Every member must contribute something critical without which the team probably cannot succeed. Every member must participate in the upside and downside of that outcome. In other words, they all must be "at risk" in the opportunity.

   Here's a deal breaker of a statement: "It's easy to build a team. Once we have the money, a team will come together." First of all, this statement exhibits a fundamental misunderstanding of teamwork. Who is the "we" in that statement? Second, this passive approach to building a team is simply not what I am looking for, and I don't know any investor who is. Cash can buy a staff but not a team. A team must evolve and prove itself worthy of funding. I need to see a team that has been tested and shown itself to be cohesive before I open my checkbook. One positive sign of a team is that its members have a long history, ideally having worked together on other startups, even if they didn't work out.

2. **Do I hear a story?** When an investor considers a startup, there is not much to judge but the story and how it is told. The question is, "Am I interested in how this story ends?" If not, that's not a good sign. What, after all, is a story but the way we explain the world to ourselves? A story is a learning tool and a teaching tool. I am impressed by teams who grasp the power of story as a mechanism to understand and address the business needs of customers.

   The delivery of the story is as important as its content. Of course, the founders have to be credible and interesting, and being articulate helps. At least one member of the team should be able to articulate the vision and purpose of the startup. It's wise for a startup to put enormous resources into developing the presentation. Doing so, of course, requires a good understanding of the product, the market, and the customers. But I can't overstate the value of a team finding the story, metaphor, or narrative to frame the information quickly. That's the leap of imagination that incubators such as Y Combinator and TechStars relentlessly promote.

   I have previously introduced readers to Keen IO. The thinking behind Keen IO is not complicated. Developers of mobile applications need to track everything from page views and clicks to more subtle user behavior, such as where users came from, where they went, and how many times the app was opened and closed. Keen IO built a cloud-based analytics infrastructure that's easy to plug in and use on a pay-as-you-go basis so developers don't have to build their own.

How do you talk about aggregating and analyzing massive amounts of data in a way that is compelling, memorable, and even enchanting? That's the task the three founders of Keen IO set for themselves during their tenure at the TechStars Cloud, the fifth iteration of the TechStars franchise. Cofounder and CTO Dan Kador (whose father is the coauthor of this book) has written an excellent blog post about the evolution of the presentation, with video of the final product as well as some earlier iterations. The differences between the 2-week, 6-week, and 13-week efforts are staggering, representing the evolution of the product under guidance of the TechStars mentors. It's revealing to see the deeper way the team was challenged to think about the business during its 13-week incubation.

3. **How enchanted am I?** I think every successful enterprise enchants its customers in some way, big or small. Think about the first time you picked up a Rubik's Cube, listened to Michael Jackson's *Thriller*, or handled any Apple product. Enchantment may be hard to define, but we know it when we see it.

    Before he became a celebrated VC, Guy Kawasaki was Apple's original marketing evangelist. For Kawasaki, the three pillars of enchantment are likability, trustworthiness, and quality. Those are the elements I want to see in a startup. It's a high standard, and not every startup can deliver enchantment. But every startup without exception should aspire to enchantment, and if the founders can't enchant me, someone who has agreed to give them my undivided attention, then what chance do they have when it comes time to prospective customers?

4. **Do the founders describe a calling?** Some founders describe their startup as a job. In general, I don't think

founders with that attitude get very far. There are lots of jobs that are easier and more certain than going the startup route. Jobs are good, but they are usually a path to something else that the worker finds fulfilling. A startup must be intrinsically fulfilling. It's almost impossible to sustain the dedication and intensity required for startup success if you think of it as a job. Other founders— sometimes called serial entrepreneurs—describe the startup route as a career. They can often be good bets for angel investors because they tend to cash out early and plunge back in again. But if I have my druthers, I prefer to invest in founders who describe their startup as a calling.

When I hear founders describe the startup path as a calling, I smile because I know they will find the work intrinsically fulfilling. Such founders are not going the startup route as a means to something else; they see their work as the end in itself, with the effort playing a role in some larger enterprise.

That's the kind of team I want to bet on, because when they think of their efforts as a calling, such founders will have frequent experiences of effortless innovation during the work day and will neither watch the clock nor look forward to knocking off early on Friday to pursue their hobbies. In fact, many such founders live where they work, the better to integrate every aspect of their lives for the success of the startup. When a startup team laboring under the influence of a common vision sprints toward their authentic calling with reckless abandon, obstacles melt away and their startup often blossoms into prosperity.

I suppose I'm drawn to founders who describe their enterprise as a calling because I like to think I have a calling, too. I pursue my own calling by passionately backing passionate entrepreneurs who have big ideas for distributing ideas on creativity and innovation throughout the world. I am committed to deploying early stage investing to maximize human capital through my investments as well as through mentoring, lecturing, and stewardship. I do these things to contribute, not just to receive, and I know it's a calling because I'd probably do it even if I didn't receive.

5. **Is the team also focused on significant wealth creation?** I ask every team what it is they want to accomplish. Some teams want to perfect a piece of technology. Some want to change the world. Some want to build large organizations. All worthy goals. But if I don't hear something explicit about creating significant wealth, I get concerned. That said, I also get concerned if money is the *only* thing I hear. I think a business needs to have a larger social purpose, but founders need to remember that, to be fundable, businesses must also be in the business of wealth creation.

6. **Is there technical or commercial competence?** I'm looking for evidence that the team has the minimal technical or commercial domain expertise to validate its approach. The ideal evidence, of course, is that the team has executed a startup before. If someone from the PayPal or Twitter development team comes to me, I'll pull out my checkbook before they are finished with their spiel. They've already proven they can do a world-class startup. But since 98 percent of the opportunities angel investors consider involve first-time entrepreneurs, the investor must determine that the team has developed the appropriate skills necessary to execute on the stated vision of the company.

Technical skills count for a lot, but many founders make the mistake of overemphasizing how smart they are and lose the perspective of the guy on the other side of the table. That would be me, the investor, wondering, "Are these guys ever going to exit?"

7. **Does the team know its numbers cold?** I'm referring to the metrics that angels expect founders to present. Every successful team I've ever encountered deeply understood the metrics of their market and knew how to measure success from the customer's point of view.

   You must be data-driven and have an impeccable handle on your metrics. Do you understand the assumptions and metrics about your market or at least have a solid understanding of how to acquire this information quickly and economically?

   I don't require founders to know everything they need to know in advance. I respect a healthy degree of ignorance. When you drive a car at night, you can see only the couple of hundred feet of roadway illuminated by the headlights. But you can make the whole trip that way.

8. **Is the team focused on execution?** Talk is cheap and everyone has big ideas, but the ability to actually implement something in a world of constraints is actually pretty rare and is something I admire, even if the execution is flawed and the enterprise fails. Startups aren't for everyone. People seem to think that startups are sexy and fun—and they can be!—but the reality is that for much of the time, they are a lot of frustration and unrelenting work. There is no place to hide in a startup.

9. **How resilient is the team?** Resilience isn't a concept you hear mentioned by too many angels, but it's a useful way to think about a team's ability to persevere.

   On the most basic level, resilience refers to an individual's capacity to cope with stress and adversity. Teams can also be said to have resilience. A resilient team has a superior ability to survive major shocks and spontaneously generate new order afterwards. Given that it's inevitable that every startup will face multiple setbacks, I wonder about the resilience of the startups I fund. Following a setback, will the team simply be defeated, will it bounce back to its previous state of functioning, or will it by some ineffable grace function better than it did before? What is it that allows some people to be knocked down by life and come back stronger than ever?

Rather than allowing setbacks to defeat them and exhaust their resolve, resilient people find a way to go from defeat to strength. A startup composed of individuals with this ability punches above its weight and will tend to do well.

10. **Is there a capacity for resolving conflicts?** It's the nature of startups to be made up of headstrong Type A individuals. Conflict among such individuals is inevitable and perhaps even desirable. It's in the collision of many ideas from superior intellects that radical innovation often flows. But not every opportunity for conflict is sublime. Every set of founders faces decisions bound to create conflict over issues that are more mundane though no less significant for the success of the business: raise or lower prices, hire or outsource, buy or lease, sell or refinance, pivot or persist, reduce costs or invest?

But one thing is certain: unresolved conflicts will distract, delay, derail, and sometimes destroy startups. As an investor, I need to have confidence that the founders have evolved healthy strategies for managing healthy conflict within the team. I look primarily for two things: a sense of humor and a willingness to deal with conflict openly.

A team that can laugh its way through conflict is a very hopeful sign. As long as it's open and above board, most conflict is manageable. Such teams use their differences to build a stronger product or business. The ability of a founder to defuse a conflict with humor sometimes suggests how a dauntingly complex problem may be divided into smaller tasks. Even if a joke does nothing more than to signal when it's time for the team to take a break, it will have done its work.

I certainly don't want to see founders arguing with each during the pitch. That's a sign you are not ready for prime time. But once the financing is out of the way, I expect the team to have disagreements and conflict. Successful teams figure out a way to openly address disagreements and resolve them. It's only when conflict is hidden or denied that things explode into endless bickering or, worse, backbiting.

CHAPTER 12 TAKEAWAYS

- Teammanship refers to the quality of the team behind the startup.

- The first element of teammanship is the leader.

- Teammanship is mostly determined by attitudes and shared values of team members.

- A group of founders does not necessarily constitute a team.

- A team is a group of equals, united by a vision, who have come together to pursue a common outcome.

Getting to No Is Just as Important as Getting to Yes

In sales, the next best thing to a "yes" is a "no." Smart startups know that only a small percentage of the angels they approach will eventually invest in them. The trick is to limit your resources to the angels who are most likely to invest and cut your losses with the rest, no matter how many questions you answer or how many documents you provide.

"Time is the most precious resource you have," says Justin Smithline, CEO of FunnelFire. "Don't squander it by pursuing angel investors who will never fund your startup."

"The 'slow no' is the worst," agrees Keen IO's Dan Kador. Startups have to vet angels even more diligently than some angels vet startups. "Know the angels who are likely to fund you by virtue of the timely investments they have funded in the past," he says. It helps if you narrow your focus to angels who, based on past investments, are a good fit for your product or service. Doing so will help you avoid unfruitful conversations in the first place.

Here's a test. Can you articulate why you are approaching a particular angel? If you can't make a good argument based on real and recent facts, you are probably wasting time for everyone involved. But if you can, it will make it easier for the angel to understand how he might relate his experience to the opportunity and speed up his evaluation to a hard yes or hard no.

Angels don't make the task easy. We have absolutely no economic incentive to say no. Maybe next week the startup will suddenly become more attractive. Why limit our options? Besides, most angels tend to be agreeable types who don't like criticizing or disappointing people who come to them for help. The result? We hem and haw and say maybe a lot. In doing so, we do startups no favors. Since most angels are historically reluctant to say no, smart entrepreneurs have to ask for it.

There are some proven strategies that usually do the trick. One is to ask the question, "What is your major hesitation about investing in us?" The angel will be relieved to hear the question framed that way, because it subtly changes the conversation from the startup's deficiencies to the angel's hesitation. So just listen to the answer. If the response has merit, then take it as a no and move on.

Another is to give the angel a deadline: "Our round is closing at noon on [insert date]. We need a decision by then. Can you help us?" Notice, the direct appeal for help? Angels are all about helping. Of course, this approach must be supported by good evidence that you'll meet all your funding requirements by that date. You'll lose all credibility and your startup will be seen as damaged goods if the deadline slips.

IT'S ABOUT TIME

Time is your most important asset. Don't spend time with people who won't advance your cause. You need to be ready and in control—and that means having control of information, timing, and process. If you can use your time wisely, angels will appreciate it. We don't want our time wasted, either.

To get a quick yes or no from Gabriel Weinberg, angel investor and CEO of DuckDuckGo, make sure the basic parameters of the investment are front and center. That includes exactly how much you are raising, how much is confirmed, when the round is closing, what terms are defined, and other essential points. "Investors usually have a funding range in which they operate, and your requirements may be out of that range—either too high or too low—immediately," Weinberg says.

After that, Weinberg wants to hear a story. A short story, he notes. The story should include a brief history of the founders, a narrative of how and why the startup was founded, and a brief summary of the vision for the startup. Weinberg says he looks for founders to nail four specific ideas:

* **What will it take to get this business to $1 to $3 million in revenue?** This part of the story shows you've thought about how this revenue level could be possible, how many customers you'd need, how much they might pay/convert/ draw in/whatever, etc. None of it needs to be correct, but it needs to be plausible. If you already have some traction, perfect—use that as a lead-in.

* **What are the possible medium and longer-term exit opportunities?** This part of the story shows you under- stand your space, how you align strategically with it, and how big you're thinking. Again, be plausible. Anything else is a red flag.

* **What about your team says you can execute on this?** This part of the story shows you personally, and I'd get really personal.

* **Why are you raising money?** Every story needs an ending, and this is usually it. "We're trying to hit this milestone by doing A, B, and C. That milestone is important because of X, Y, and Z."

DESERVE A QUICK NO

"Entrepreneurs deserve a quick no," agrees angel investor Linda Holliday. "If angels are not going to invest, then they are wasting the founder's time, and that's all they have, so it's not fair to waste it."

Holliday also subscribes to a view that is increasingly rare among angel investors. She believes that entrepreneurs deserve to hear exactly why she declines to invest. I tend to agree. Normally, when I reject an opportunity, I think it's fair that I give the entrepreneurs at least one constructive piece of information about their presentation or idea. *No* should come with a *because*.

Let me confess something here. Although I agree with Linda, I don't always follow her advice because I don't have time for arguments. Linda Holliday understands why some angels are reluctant to get into giving reasons for declining an opportunity to invest. "Some entrepreneurs are immature, and they get resentful or emotional because I criticized their baby," she says. "Angels don't want a scene, so they back off. As a result, even people who are open to that incredibly valuable feedback don't get it."

Sometimes the people who ask for feedback and promise to use it responsibly break their promise. My coauthor John Kador tells a story about buying a car. A knowledgeable, young sales rep showed John a few cars, and John was ready to shake hands on the deal. But then the sales rep offended John with an off-putting, stupid joke, and John backed away from the deal and left the showroom. Later that evening, the sales rep called John.

"Please help me," the salesman said. "I assume I did or said something wrong, but I have no idea what it is. I really need some honest feedback here. Can you tell me what I did so I can learn for next time?"

In a situation like that, I'd be willing to tell the sales rep the truth. Like most angels, I'm eager to help entrepreneurs improve their game. But John is perhaps a better judge of character. I'll let him continue the story:

> I decided to give the salesperson the benefit of the doubt. Maybe he was asleep in sales school when they said to save the jokes until after the contract is signed. Most of all, I didn't want an argument. So here's what I told him: "I'll give you the feedback you asked for, but on three conditions."
>
> "Anything," the salesman quickly replied.
>
> "The first condition is that you do not interrupt me. The second condition is that you do not defend yourself. The third condition is that you do not contact me again for six months," I said. "Do I have your agreement?"
>
> The phone was silent for about three seconds, replaced by a dial tone. He hung up on me.

Angel investor Alain Bankier also wants to tell startups why he doesn't think it makes sense for him to invest. Sometimes they listen respectfully, but some actually argue with him. He recently met with a team of super-smart engineers working on a startup in a space that Alain knows and likes. But the team sought a valuation that Alain thought was unrealistic.

"I kept telling the team that the valuation doesn't make sense, that the value isn't there yet, that the proposed approach will cause increasing problems in the capital structure down the road. I added that I would be delighted to invest at a lower number. The team kept arguing for the higher number and even got an unexperienced seed investment at the higher valuation. 'Others are doing it,' they implored. 'Why can't you?' All I could do was say no and tell them exactly why. Unfortunately for them, just as I predicted, the next round was a down round and it created a lot of issues, both for the early investors as well as the entrepreneurs."

CHAPTER 13 TAKEAWAYS

- Only a small percentage of angels will invest, so focus on the angels most likely to say yes.

- Can you articulate why you are approaching a particular angel?

- Angels have absolutely no economic incentive to say no.

- Entrepreneurs deserve a quick decision, so ask for it.

- Ask the angel to articulate his or her objections.

- Ask for feedback; listen but don't argue.

Iterating the Startup   14

Iterating the startup is about increasing the startup's chances of securing angel funding.

Iteration has been proven to be a successful approach to the challenges of launching a business. A similar approach can be applied to raising seed capital. In many ways, the process of raising money has many parallels to the process of acquiring customers and making a sale. The only difference is that with raising money, the product you are selling is incremental in your company.

In one important way, iterating a startup for raising money is easier than iterating it to make sales. When the iteration is designed to attract funding, you only need to make a handful of sales to the handful of angel investors whom you want in your round.

ITERATION VS. PIVOT

Some readers might confuse iteration with the pivot, a concept that has taken on a mythic, almost religious significance.

Pivoting is a radical change of the current business model or product in an attempt to capitalize on a new and different market opportunity. Iteration is an incremental change of the current business model or product in an attempt to capitalize on a tightly related market opportunity. The pivot is usually wrenching, risky, and expensive. Pivoting often takes significant time to execute; iteration can be implemented in minutes.

Raising seed money for your startup is not easy. It's hard to know what will get traction with investors. Entrepreneurs have learned to iterate every aspect of the business, from the business model to the product design and marketing messages. Systematic trial and error becomes embedded in every aspect of the innovation life cycle for the simple reason that it's cheaper and more flexible than investing everything in one initiative.

Iteration refers to the act of repeating a process, usually with the aim of approaching a desired goal. The result of each iteration forms the basis or starting point for the next one. In this way, a series of iterations allows you to quickly test ideas, gather feedback, and develop new approaches, all in an endless quest for improvement. Iteration is a quintessentially fact-based process; there's no room for sentimentality or wishful thinking. I've mentioned before that the facts are friendly (not always convenient, but always worth knowing). Testing against reality is the ultimate way to answer the myriad questions facing startups every day; an iterative approach allows reality to be tested quickly, economically, and with the stakes lowered for all concerned.

It may be that the first iteration of your startup will fail to get the attention of angels. If so, maybe your approach needs to be tweaked.

There are books describing how to iterate established businesses or products in order to improve them. These are absolutely critical skills for entrepreneurs to have, and I look for evidence of them. But in this chapter, I want to discuss being flexible enough to iterate the very conception of the business and the way it's presented.

ATTRACTIVE TO ANGELS

For entrepreneurs, the object of iteration is to raise money by making the business attractive to angels. I generally see businesses before they have a product to iterate. At first, most startups are half-baked. Before the startup launches, much will change. That's why I need to see evidence that the startup team has the ability to adapt quickly to changing conditions. The benefits of doing so include:

- **Faster funding.** I respect teams that demonstrate an ability to iterate. But I fund startups that demonstrate an eagerness to iterate. I love startups that show a hunger for collecting information, analyzing it without preconditions, and adjusting their startup model until they have it right.

- **Faster time to market.** By iterating your product development and launch, you can generate satisfied customers in weeks or months instead of years. Market conditions change quickly. Even if you get your target right at the beginning, it's likely the target will move or shift. Iteration provides the best way to adjust the startup for continued relevance.

- **Get traction before funding.** Angels love to see evidence that a startup actually has a product or service that real customers are paying for. By iterating their startup model, entrepreneurs may actually generate a prototype that attracts a handful of customers. Angels perk up their ears when they hear about revenue. Where you might see a tiny revenue stream, most angels will see a mighty river.

- **Identify customers, partners, and channels.** There is nothing like a real customer pipeline with demonstrated customer acquisition costs to persuade angels to open their checkbooks.

ITERATION IS THE NEW INNOVATION

When I started out in the business world, there was a lot less iteration. Entrepreneurs would start with a business idea, leave their conventional job, and try to make the business a success. If it worked out, great. If it didn't, necessity would force them back into the nine-to-five job market. Maybe they might try the startup route again a few years later. But today, if a startup isn't successful, entrepreneurs start iterating various aspects of the business, trying different permutations until they succeed, even if the business they end up with is quite different than the business they started with. Most entrepreneurs assume they won't get it right the first time.

In a celebrated essay called "Startups in 13 Sentences," Y Combinator's Paul Graham talks about iteration in terms of customer satisfaction. One of Graham's key points is that launching teaches entrepreneurs what they should have been building all along. He suggested that it's better to make a few customers really happy than to make a lot of customers semi-happy. His essay helped usher in the era of agile iterative software development methodology, in which customer solutions evolve as developers learn more about customer requirements and changing market conditions.

Out of this thinking flowed the concept of the minimum viable product (MVP) popularized by Eric Ries. According to Ries, an MVP embraces just those features that allow the product to be deployed, and no more. "The MVP is that version of a new product which allows a team to collect the maximum amount of validated learning about customers with the least effort," he says. The MVP is typically rolled out to a subset of potential customers thought likely to grasp the potential of the product and believed to be eager to provide feedback. The goal is to build only the product that customers actually need. MVPs are about generating information more than about generating sales.

The MVP, then, is less a product than an iterative strategy and learning tool. The process is iterated until a desirable product-market fit is obtained, or until the product is abandoned in favor of something totally different and the process begins again.

I love startups that demonstrate an iterative foundation in product development. I get excited by teams that intend to build the smallest kernel of their central concept, roll it out for the world to taste, see how the market reacts to it, and then improve, improve, improve. I've seen teams make spectacular progress with this approach.

Yet I have also seen teams falter with it. Basically, entrepreneurs with the mindset of "see what happens and do it more" tend to give up too quickly.

The MVP process is successful for discrete products, especially engineering-intensive products such as hardware. But if the market doesn't immediately respond, startups tend to move on to the next big thing. "If there's a delay in pickup from the community, it's easy to move on to the next thing, the next launch, the next hoopla, as opposed to doing the insanely hard work of sticking with that thing you already launched," says marketing guru Seth Godin. That's because marketing plays by different rules than engineering. "Many products depend on community, on adoption within a tribe, on buzz," he says.

ITERATE IS A VERB

Iteration is intensively action-focused, but that doesn't mean you don't plan. It means, rather, that you aren't invested in the plan being perfect. Indeed, the assumption is that the plan is flawed.

Nevertheless, without a plan, iterating is fruitless. I totally reject the approach of "throwing things against the wall to see what will stick." That's not a strategy to inspire any angel.

Iteration can be a great friend to startups. It's particularly beneficial when you're starting in a line of business in which your team has experience. There are six characteristics of iteration for a startup.

- **Develop a hypothesis.** The hypothesis is a statement that explains why your idea or business will be attractive to angel investors. If the hypothesis gets traction, it will likely inform your elevator pitch and then form the basis of your business plan, should you get to that stage.

- **It's the feedback, stupid.** Entrepreneurs often assume they are smarter about their startups than they actually are. Better to start stupid and let the iteration educate you. Markets will always humble entrepreneurs who fail to listen. The key is to listen to what customers are telling you. This is not as easy as it sounds, because users will rarely articulate what they want or don't want. Rather, you have to observe how they use the product. Pay enough attention and users will show you most of what you need to know about the feature mix, the value proposition, and the pricing model. It's infernally difficult to forecast what customers will pay for until they actually pull out their wallets.

- **Test and retest the hypothesis.** Get out of the building and talk to as many prospects as possible. Talk to anyone who will listen as early in the process as you can. This is the time to fail fast.

- **Don't shoot your wad in the first iteration.** You'll need to reserve resources for the second, third, and subsequent iterations. Overspending on the first iteration is the most common mistake startups make. It's perfectly understandable. You are excited and want to hit a home run, so you swing for the fences. But the point of iteration is just to get on base. That means starting lean. I know it's frustrating for startups to leave off all those services and features that will no doubt resonate with customers. But that's a goal for a different day. Right now, the point is to launch sooner, saving time and money, and gather feedback.

- **Reflect fearlessly.** It's pointless to collect information and feedback if you're not going to reflect on what it all means and then make adjustments. Unfortunately, too many startups are so absorbed in the relentless grind of putting out fires that they never quite get around to considering what all that feedback indicates. I'm a big advocate of founders periodically getting away from the routine for a day or two to consider the larger themes of the startup. I'm impressed by a team that can say something like, "At the team's second strategic offsite retreat, we decided . . ." I'm usually less interested in the specific decision than the fact that the team took the time to reflect and plan.

- **Take action.** All the reflection in the world does no good unless you actually take action. The critical thing is to act on what you've learned so that the next iteration is incrementally better than the last.

I'm willing to make myself available for this type of feedback, and I know most of my fellow New York Angels are, too. This is exactly how we build our brands and improve the quality of the deal flow all angels seek.

If your idea has a fatal flaw, would you rather know it in 45 days or in four years? That's the promise of iteration. It doesn't often change the outcome, it just makes the outcome quicker.

The iteration model can lower risks and take some of the pressure off you as your startup seeks early-stage funding. You'll certainly get some things wrong, but that's okay—as long as you learn quickly and try again. It may take a few iterations, but each cycle will get you closer to a fundable product or business. Or not. Sometimes it becomes clear that the business is not scalable, a competitor is too strong, or the market is too amorphous. In such cases, you get to walk away without having invested too much time or resources. But if you have the kernel of a good idea for a business, with hard work, smart decisions, and committed angels, you will have a good shot at succeeding.

CHAPTER 14 TAKEAWAYS

- Iteration can be used to make a startup more attractive to angels.

- Iterate is a verb.

- Iteration is the new innovation.

- Pivot and iteration are different.

Baking in the Exit from the Beginning

Every startup should start with an exit strategy. Entrepreneurs do well to remember that the two sweetest words to an angel investor's ears are "liquidity event." They're not bad for entrepreneurs, either.

A startup's exit strategy should be signed off on by the founders before seeking dollar one of external financing. A well-crafted exit strategy, aligned to the characteristics of the startup and market conditions, will improve the probability of success, shorten the time to exit, and often increase the ultimate valuation at exit.

Early exits are attractive for both angels and entrepreneurs. An exit event is the only way angels get paid. "Looking at it in the simplest terms, or as an investor would, the company is simply a black box with the inputs being entrepreneurs' effort and investors' cash and the only output being the purchase price paid by the ultimate buyer," says J. Basil Peters, a British Columbia angel who lectures, blogs, and has written the definitive book on the topic of early exits.

For entrepreneurs, early exits translate into new opportunities. These days, companies are often sold only two or three years after they're founded. YouTube sold was just two years old when Google bought it for $1.6 billion. Flickr was a year and half old when Yahoo bought it for $30 million. Instagram was also just two years old when Facebook acquired it for $1 billion. In 2005, a startup called iStockphoto emerged as a leading source of crowd-sourced images. Getty Images, the 800-pound gorilla of the stock photo market, bought it for $50 million. Since then, Getty has bought more than 100 other photo collections and companies.

There's a myth that you have to grow a company to a certain size or profit level to have a decent exit. But today the real threshold is just to prove the business model of the company works. You really need just two data points. If you can establish, one, the lifetime value of a customer and, two, the acquisition costs for that customer, you and I can have a good conversation about valuation.

A number of things are going on here. First, the costs of starting a business are getting lower every day. When I started investing, businesses needed at least $5 million to get off the ground. Now I see viable businesses being formed for $200,000. Second, the Internet allows companies to build startups literally over a weekend. In so-called "weekenders," teams build entire Web-based businesses—from concept to launch to revenue—in one Red Bull–infused, no-sleep session. Before the sun dawns on Monday morning, a few of these teams even succeed in selling the startup. The Internet has compressed what used to take two years, or two quarters, into a little more than two days, another example of Moore's law in action.

Startup Weekends are 54-hour events where developers, designers, marketers, product managers, and startup enthusiasts come together to share ideas, form teams, build products, and launch startups. The teams have a good idea if their startups are viable by the end of the event. Beginning with open mic pitches on Friday, attendees bring their best ideas and inspire others to join their team. Over Saturday and Sunday, teams focus on customer development, validating their ideas, practicing Lean Startup methodologies, and building a minimal viable product.

On Sunday evening, teams demo their prototypes and receive valuable feedback from a panel of experts.

Yes, most startups today still take more than two years to achieve an optimum exit, but the trend is toward quicker, not slower, exits. The metabolism of startups is accelerating every day. Some of the weekend startups may be little more than learning experiments or opportunities to meet other entrepreneurs, but according to Startup Weekends, 36 percent of its startups are still being developed three months later. Startup Weekends cost between $75 and $99 and include access to mentors, meals, and all the coffee you can drink.

THE BUSINESS PROCESS THAT PAYS OFF MOST

The exit is really just another business process—along with product development and marketing—that the startup team must master. "The biggest difference," says Basil Peters, "is that the exit process often makes more money for the shareholders than any other process during the company's lifetime. Designing and executing the exit well can easily increase the entire value of the business by 50 percent or more."

If you understand that, you'll understand the fixation all angels have with exits. And then you won't be surprised, as you're pitching me about your brand-new startup, when I ask you to talk about your exit strategy. I know that's a painful thought for entrepreneurs. They are often shocked that I would ask such a question. This is typical of the wounded rejoinders: "Exit strategy? You want to hear about our exit strategy? We haven't even started the company yet, and you're talking about selling it?"

And the answer is, yes, absolutely. I want to know from day one how you intend to architect the exit. I need to know you see the writing on the wall.

I understand that many startups are not focused on the exit because they are focused on building the company, growing market share, and getting profitable. Those are excellent goals, but not if you want funding from angel investors. Why? Because the analysis is clear: the bigger a company gets, the chances for a successful exit actually decrease.

It's just so much easier to get acquired when you're relatively small. The prices are usually in the $10 to $25 million range. There are more decision-makers with the authority to make acquisitions at that level. But if a company becomes bigger in size, market share, and profits, possibilities for exits narrow. First of all, competitors will certainly challenge you. As the price to acquire you goes up, acquisitions become more expensive and consequently more complex.

That's why angels want to understand the exit before they invest. When a startup with a half decent idea can show that the exit is clear and well positioned, angels quickly pull out their checkbooks. Here's an example of what I mean.

One day the New York Angels saw a presentation from an entrepreneur who wanted to change the way people searched for and watched movies on TV. Many startups are born in response to a particular frustration. This was a little frustration, and the entrepreneur admitted it. "I just want to change the world a little bit, and then I want an early exit," he told us. He identified a number of TV publications and cable TV companies that could use his product as a front end for their own viewing marketplace. Moreover, he demonstrated a prototype, offered a term sheet that made the marketplace very clear to us, and offered a valuation that was more than fair.

What happened next is pretty much unheard of. Within 90 minutes of meeting him, we funded him for nearly $100,000. We actually wrote checks around the table. I don't recommend this approach, but in this case the presentation, grounded in the early exit, was too compelling to pass up. And we were right. Within

18 months, the startup was acquired by a company that manufactures set-top boxes for TVs. The participating angels received a little more than three times their investment, a return made appetizing by the extremely quick exit.

As I mentioned in the introduction, my son Trace and I developed Launch.it, a platform for information about new products and services to have a home where it can be found, where it can be shared, where it can be discovered and even purchased or funded. We wanted to remove all friction from the activity of getting visibility for every new product in a world of innovation and creativity. One of the first things we did was consider the established companies that might find Launch.it attractive if we demonstrated its potential.

We had a theory. Even though a wire service that handles traditional new product announcements might find the idea of Launch.it attractive, they couldn't build such a platform because it would be so disruptive to their existing business model. But they might buy it if someone else developed it. Not three months after our startup launch, we had an opportunity to test our theory. It wasn't hard for us to get appointments with the wire services.

If I were an angel investor in my own startup (and I guess I am), I would tell myself, "Launch.it is probably a good investment, because I know that a number of billion-dollar companies that are so big they cannot get out of their own way will see this product as either a revenue source or as a disruption to their existing revenue and will want to buy it."

TWO EXITS

There are really only two types of exits available for a startup company: selling the company (being acquired) or going public in an IPO. The former is much, much more likely than the latter. Frankly, the math from IPOs doesn't make sense, and after the Facebook IPO fiasco, investors are shying away. Of every 1,000 startups angels invest in that eventually exit, 999 will be acquired.

So the real question becomes, "Is there an entity that will desire the products or services that your startup is building?"

If you can show me that you've identified a target and created the conditions to make a logical acquisition, then, my friend, you have my undivided attention. Let me see that you're baking in the exit from the beginning.

Angel investor Alain Bankier, introduced in Chapter 5, got his start in investment banking and mergers and acquisitions, which taught him to focus on the exit from Day One. "Before I invest in a startup, I like to know that the team has not only thought about the end game, but is willing to consider the end game as part of the ongoing business process," he says.

What does it mean to prepare a company for the end game? It means waking up every day and running the business like you are getting ready to sell it or bring in new investors. It means asking, "In terms of legal structure and reporting structure, have we done everything to make the company as attractive as possible? Are we always thinking about building shareholder value? Are the financials as understandable and transparent as possible? Are they audited? Can we demonstrate the value proposition of the startup in terms that partners, vendors, and, especially, customers can understand?

THE ACQUI-HIRE

Also known as the HR acquisition, the acqui-hire refers to an established company buying a startup primarily for its engineering or, rarely, marketing talent. The startup's technology may be folded into the established company's portfolio, or it may be discarded. The startup itself is invariably shut down. Such transactions, typically in the $2 to $6 million range, are becoming more commonplace as demand for software engineers has soared.

The good news about an acqui-hire is that it's an exit, which is better than bankruptcy. It allows the entrepreneur to save face by saying, "I sold my company to Google." But most founders think of the acqui-hire as the exit of last resort. For entrepreneurs, accepting an acqui-hire signals that their dream of starting a business of their own is dead. For employees who are not part of the package, an acqui-hire means unemployment. For angel investors, an acqui-hire often results in low or even zero returns.

The motives of the acquiring company are clear. Building effective teams from scratch is difficult and time-consuming. An acqui-hire of a team that has proven it can design, build, and deliver a product has many benefits. It allows the acquired team to stay together and work on important projects with the additional resources and weight of the big company behind them.

Companies that need to move fast know that it's easier to acquire a team that knows an industry rather than to launch a new business unit and learn as they go.

The benefits to the entrepreneurs themselves are seen only in the context of the alternative. Usually, these companies are out of money and momentum. The founders, who may not have taken a salary in years, are frequently in dire financial straits. So the job security, signing bonuses, decent salary, and benefits begin to look attractive. You also get to say you've had a successful exit, which looks good if you decide to try another startup in the future.

Few angels think of an acqui-hire exit as desirable. True, angels can declare that another one of their startups was acquired by Google or Facebook, but they know that measured by financial results, such exits represent a breakeven at best and a total loss of investment at worst. Investors call it a "soft" exit. Many VCs actively discourage their startups from going the acqui-hire route, while others help set up acqui-hires for their struggling startups since everybody loses in a bankruptcy. My own view is that if an acqui-hire is the best option for the founders, I'm not going to get in their way.

WHOSE EXIT STRATEGY IS IT ANYWAY?

When it comes time to get acquired, everyone looks to the usual suspects: Google, Facebook, Apple, Amazon, and others, including many established companies that you might not think of. The reality is that many of these companies are in the market for the talent and sometimes the disruptive products that startups represent.

In 2011, Google made 79 acquisitions, mostly small companies for their IP or engineering talent. Yes, Google paid $12.5 billion for Motorola Mobility, but that was an exception. Ninety percent of its acquisitions were for startups with valuations of less than $20 million and fewer than 20 employees. According to insiders, Google actually prefers to acquire companies that are prerevenue.

An effective exit strategy doesn't have to be complicated. For example, I recently heard from a startup that articulated its exit strategy in one sentence: "At our third strategic planning retreat, the entire team agreed that our central strategic goal was to sell the company in about four years for more than $15 million."

Perfect. A target date and a target price is all I really need. I accept that it's unlikely for either objective to be realized. But it's enormously reassuring for me to know that the team has considered the matter of the exit and is aligned around a set of targets. I was also impressed that the team had at least three strategic retreats.

It's always best to sell a company on its promise, not its reality. Stuff happens, and in my experience, that stuff is never good. There's a lot of stuff that can go wrong, so get out early.

I've seen too many entrepreneurs leave money on the table because they waited too long to exit. When that happens it's usually because the company is doing well, market share and revenues are increasing, the press is great, and everyone is excited. It's great to see the run-up. But the reality is that the best time to sell is often when business metrics are on the upward trend. What usually happens is the founders wait until the company is at its peak, and by the time the sale is ready, the company is no longer at its peak value.

CHAPTER 15 TAKEAWAYS

- Every startup should start with an exit strategy.

- Angels look to invest in startups that can demonstrate an exit strategy.

- An exit event is the only way angel investors get paid.

- The cost of launching startups is getting lower.

- Some businesses are being created in a weekend.

- In an acqui-hire (HR acquisition), an established company buys a startup primarily for its engineering talent.

Due Diligence
Checklist

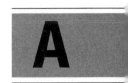

This is the due diligence checklist developed by the New York Angels. Just like a pilot goes through a preflight checklist before taking off, we at the New York Angels find that unless we formalize the process, some important piece is usually overlooked.

Deal Lead _____   **Target Completion Date** _____

	Due Date	Status	NYA Review Responsibility	NYA Review Due Date	NYA Review Status
Corporate					
Cap table (w/ESOP)					
Board of directors (bios)					
Corporate docs (cert of inc, etc…)					
Historical financing terms					
Future financing strategy					
Management/board of advisors					
Reference checks					
1 _____					
2 _____					
3 _____					
Mnmgt résumés					
Organizational plan					
Business model					
Business plan					
Target customer					

	NYA Review				
	Due Date	Status	Responsibility	Due Date	Status
Revenue streams					
Market data (relevant segment)					
Competitive comparison					
Future growth plan					
Sales and marketing plan					
Strategic alliances/affiliations					
Contracts					
Reference					
Proof of concept (sales by customer)					
Customer reference checks					
1 ____					
2 ____					
Sales presentation to customer					
Financial					
Financial model					
Cash flow statement					
Balance sheet					
Operating expense detail					

(continued on next page)

	Due Date	Status	NYA Review		
			Responsibility	Due Date	Status
3- to 5-year projections					
Income statement					
Burn rate by month					
Gross margin by product					
Product/service					
Market research					
Samples/access					
Technology description					
Operations					
List of business partners					
Legal					
IP					
Trademarks					
Regulatory					
Litigation					
Deal terms					
Valuation					

	NYA Review					
	Due Date	Status	Responsibility	Due Date	Status
Exit target and multiples					
Term sheet					
Use of funds/milestones					
Other					

The New York Angels Term Sheet

B

This is the term sheet developed by the New York Angels. Other angels and angel groups have similar but unique term sheets. The final stage of the angel investing process requires finalizing the terms of the deal. A topline discussion of valuation will have already occurred at the start of due diligence. The key components of the term sheet will be the amount of money to be raised and at what pre-money valuation that money will invest. Generally, the New York Angels do deals in the range of $100,000 to $1.0 million and at pre-money valuations less than $5 million. The term sheet will contain other protective provisions common in angel investing and may include a board seat.

For more information about terms, check out the term sheet definition worksheet on the Angel Capital Association website (www.angelcapitalassociation.org). Also, law firm Wilson Sonsini (www.wsgr.com) has an interactive term sheet generator that makes understanding term sheets easy.

TERMS FOR PRIVATE PLACEMENT
OF SEED SERIES PREFERRED STOCK OF
[*INSERT COMPANY NAME*], INC.

[Date]

The following is a summary of the principal terms with respect to the proposed Seed Series Preferred Stock financing of _____, Inc., a [Delaware] corporation (the "*Company*"). Except for the sections entitled "Expenses", "No Shop/Confidentiality" [and "Special Terms"], such summary of terms does not constitute a legally binding obligation. Any other legally binding obligation will only be made pursuant to definitive agreements to be negotiated and executed by the parties.

Offering Terms

Securities to Issue:	Shares of Seed Series Preferred Stock of the Company (the "*Series Seed*").
Aggregate Proceeds:	Minimum of $_____ [and maximum of $_____ in aggregate].
Lead Investors:	Members of New York Angels, Inc. who will invest a minimum of $_____
Price Per Share:	$_____ (the "*Original Issue Price*"), based on a pre-money valuation of $_____, calculated based upon the capitalization of the Company as set forth in Exhibit A and an available post-closing option pool of 15% after receipt of maximum Aggregate Proceeds.
Dividends:	Annual 6% accruing cumulative dividend payable when as and if declared, and upon (a) a Redemption or (b) a Liquidation (including a Deemed Liquidation Event) of

the Company in which the holders of Series Seed receive less than 5 times the Original Issue Price per share (the "Cap"). For any other dividends or distributions, participation with Common Stock on an as-converted basis.

Liquidation Preference: One times the Original Issue Price plus any accrued and unpaid dividends thereon (subject to the "Cap") plus any other declared but unpaid dividends on each share of Series Seed, balance of proceeds paid to Common. A merger, consolidation, reorganization, sale or exclusive license of all or substantially all of the assets or similar transaction in one or a series of related transactions will be treated as a liquidation (a "Deemed Liquidation Event").

Conversion: Convertible into one share of Common (subject to proportional adjustments for stock splits, stock dividends and the like, and Full Ratchet anti-dilution protection if securities are sold for capital raising purposes at less than 75% of the valuation in this round within the first 2 years after the round) at any time at the option of the holder.

Voting Rights: Votes together with the Common Stock on all matters on an as-converted basis. Approval of a majority of the Series Seed required to (i) adversely change rights of the Series Seed; (ii) change the authorized number of shares; (iii) authorize a new series of Preferred Stock having rights senior to or on parity with the Series Seed; (iv) create or authorize the creation of any debt security if the Company's aggregate indebtedness would exceed 50% of the aggregate proceeds of the Series Seed; (v) redeem or repurchase any shares (other than pursuant to the Company's right of repurchase at original cost); (vi) declare or pay any dividend; (vii) increase in the option pool reserve within two years following the closing; (viii) change the number of directors; or (ix) liquidate or dissolve, including any change of control or Deemed Liquidation Event.

Documentation: Documents will be based on Seed Series Preferred Stock documents published at http:/gust.com/SeriesSeed which will be generated/drafted by Company counsel.

Five Indispensable Tools Founders Can Use to Do Due Diligence on Angels

LINKEDIN

LinkedIn is an extraordinary resource for general background information on investors. I don't know a single investor of significance who isn't on LinkedIn. And by the way, if you're not on LinkedIn, you should be. LinkedIn is the most popular social network for professionals, and many LinkedIn members are also active investors looking for businesses and startups to fund.

A basic membership is free. Besides, if your startup has anything to do with social media (and, these days, what doesn't?) and you're not on one of the three or four premier social networking platforms, it invites a question about your social media literacy. Nothing good can come of your absence from LinkedIn.

LinkedIn is huge. Do a search for my name and over 500 Brian Cohens come up. Depending on the individuals in your network, my profile may come up first or last or somewhere in between. But if you limit the results by using the "by location" search feature (specify "Greater New York City area"), my profile will almost certainly be first or second. A quick glance then gives you a myriad of information potentially useful to establish a connection. My education (Syracuse University, Boston University) is there. So is a bio with my career time line and milestones, a list of my recent speaking engagements, and a long list of groups and associations I am associated with.

As I said, virtually all significant angel investors have LinkedIn profiles. Take a good look at the investor's network, and look for people you know in common. Maybe you can get an introduction, which is always preferable to a cold call. But even a cold call is made a little warmer when you are able to note that you and the investor have a colleague in common.

Although LinkedIn can't guarantee that you'll find the right funding partner, get the money you need, and build your business with a great return on investment, using LinkedIn can help you improve your chances of success when dealing with the funding and growth of your business.

Moreover, LinkedIn is a tremendous resource for founders whether or not you use it to locate specific investors. LinkedIn Answers allows you to tap a vast network of expertise about all aspects of early-stage investing. Check out the Startups and Small Business subsection of LinkedIn Answers for guidance regarding private equity. You will see a targeted list of questions and answers. Sample questions other founders have asked include:

- Who should I go to for nontraditional funding of a startup?

- What's the difference between a venture capitalist and an angel investor?

- What are some good venture capital websites?

- Who are the venture capitalists who invest in scalable open source ventures?

- What is the best way to seek interim funding during a period of heavy VC negotiations?

- How do venture capitalists view venture debt before, during, and after different funding rounds?

LinkedIn members can also pose their own questions and wait for experts to respond. When you receive an answer to a question you ask on LinkedIn Answers, review the member's profile, and send a connection request. It's a great way to establish a relationship with a potential angel, and you can parlay that relationship into connections with the angel's connections. Your overarching objective on LinkedIn should always be to connect with as many angels as possible.

You can use the Financing subsection of LinkedIn Answers to get critiques or reviews of your executive summaries, directly ask for an angel investor to consider your venture, or ask other founders to evaluate their experience with a particular angel investor. Most questions, requests for advice, and direct appeals for investment usually receive multiple responses.

Your goal as a founder is to link with as many potential investors as possible. Connecting with a LinkedIn member requires you to send a connection request. I guarantee that the first thing an investor will do is to view your LinkedIn profile before accepting the request, so make sure the page describes your background and startup and highlights your accomplishments and associations. LinkedIn works by enriching the networks of people you connect with, so make the case that connecting with you will be useful to them.

Make it easy for investors to find you. By adding keywords such as *startup* or *angel investment* to your LinkedIn profile, you increase the chances that your profile will display in related searches. At the same time, make sure your profile conveys your commitment to learning, sharing, and community. Many

LinkedIn members welcome being mentors. Keep your profile active and updated. A profile with little or no activity is far less desirable to a potential angel than an extremely active profile that tells a story about a founder who is committed to learning.

LinkedIn Groups are another powerful way to meet prospective investors. One good way to identify groups you might want to join is by looking at the groups your LinkedIn connections belong to. You can search for groups the same way that you search for people, selecting "Groups" from the drop-down menu next to the search box. The search function allows you to narrow your search by keyword and geography.

Don't hesitate to join the groups that are open to everyone. After you join, study the conversation for a few days, and then jump in by asking a question or offering a resource. Check out the subgroups that are focused on specific subjects or networking. Some LinkedIn groups are open by invitation only. Every such group has a moderator, so send a message about why you want to join and what you have to offer the group. You are able to send LinkedIn messages to all group members when you join a group. This ability is gold as you try to enlarge your network of LinkedIn contacts.

GUST

An indispensable tool for startups is Gust, the global platform that is on the way to connecting all of the world's startup companies with all of the world's angel investors. That sounds like a tall order, but as of this writing, Gust is already used by over 165,000 startups to connect with over 42,000 accredited investors. It is also the platform used by over 800 organized angel groups (including New York Angels) and 300 venture capital funds to manage all of their funding applications and investment portfolios. More than just a matching service, Gust is actually building the infrastructure for the whole early-stage financing industry. It received the 2012 CODiE Award (the U.S. software industry's equivalent of the Oscars) for Best Collaboration and Social Networking Solution, and the 2012 Innotribe Award from the SWIFT international banking industry consortium as the world's most innovative financial technology company.

Gust allows entrepreneurs to create a profile for their startup that is always live and under their control. They can easily update the information as it changes, collaborate on funding, and basically have a do-it-yourself investor relations site for their startup, which supports the company from its initial approach to investors, through pitching, due diligence, investment and ongoing investor relations . . . all the way to an eventual exit. Gust also offers a powerful social media platform through which entrepreneurs can network with—and be found by—angels interested in making investments.

The power of Gust is that tens of thousands of investors around the world use the same platform for managing the investment relationship from their side of the table as well. So once you have entered your materials into your private Gust site, you may never have to fill out another application again. Gust serves as a "universal application processor" for over 85 percent of the world's organized angel groups, as well as hundreds of business plan competitions, accelerators, venture capital funds, and entrepreneurial events. Investors can filter and search through the startups listed on Gust by a wide range of criteria. Only those investors and/or mentors to whom you have specifically granted permission to access your profile will be able to see the details of your financials and progress. Gust is immensely useful at every step of the "pitch-to-exit" business life cycle.

By the way, the Gust website profiles over a dozen high-profile angel investors and features short videos of us presenting on everything from branding to failure to presentation tips. You can find my videos at http://videos.gust.com/pages/brian-cohen. Note also that Gust is integrated with Launch.it, the new product publicity platform that I founded together with my son, Trace. That means investors who see your launch material on Launch.it can directly request access to your investor materials on Gust, and your Launch.it dashboard will be accessible from directly within Gust.

In short, Gust is a must. My experience is that at least 75 percent of startups looking to raise money put their documents on Gust. But do it right. I've seen a lot of profiles on Gust that are confusing, incomplete, and amateurish. When that happens, I don't look further. So the profile has to be complete and utterly professional.

ANGELLIST

AngelList is, first and foremost, a community of startups and investors who make fund-raising efficient by matching startups who need investment with angel investors looking to invest. No longer do founders need connections or access to the "old boy's network" to find investors. AngelList levels the playing field. Like eLoan, where a borrower can pitch 10 or more banks at the same time for the best terms on a mortgage, founders can pitch 10 or more angels. Because the intros to angels are curated, the conversion rate for angels is much higher than in the analog world, where founders meet with angels one at a time. When the process works well, it can go very quickly.

The curation is what makes the site work. The site uses restrictive criteria to separate the wheat from the chaff. Only five percent of the companies that apply to be featured on AngelList are presented to angels for consideration. Angels welcome this feature, because it saves them from having to review manifestly unqualified pitches. The AngelList team selects only startups that can show some growth, have some other criteria to recommend them, or are endorsed by a known investor or industry colleague. AngelList rejects applications that are missing information. For those startups that make the cut, AngelList forwards the pitch to all the angels who have indicated an interest in that sector, such as mobile, health, or cloud computing.

The screening works both ways. AngelList also screens angel investors, requiring them to authenticate themselves and list past investments. Angels must be active. Lurkers are not welcome. If angels haven't made an investment in 12 months, they are kicked out, as are investors who've violated the rules. Startups can screen potential investors on a variety of criteria, such as specific investing experience, skills, industry, or geographical coverage.

The only prerequisite is that you need to already have at least one investor—the more conspicuous, the better. AngelList is effective for startups that already have investors and are looking to complete their round. If you have already raised some money, AngelList can be effective, and you can use it to screen and select the smartest investors possible. That saves a lot of time for everyone. Think of AngelList as another social media platform, and use it accordingly.

I think startups should try AngelList. What do you have to lose? There are investors out there listening, and if your startup shows up on AngelList with certain characteristics, they may find you and reach out.

TECHCRUNCH

TechCrunch, a web publication that offers technology news, analysis, and profiles of startups, is arguably the most influential news blog in high tech. Founded by Michael Arrington in 2005, it has become the de facto trade publication in Silicon Valley, and was acquired by AOL in 2010. For startups that score a mention, the upside can be impressive. I know a number of startups who received thousands of user signups after a TechCrunch mention. It can get you in front of a bunch of early adopters for a couple of days, and it also does wonders for your SEO, which is always useful.

So naturally, founders ask me if I can get TechCrunch to cover their startup. The answer is no, and even if I could, that's your job, not mine. Still, here are a few tips that can't steer you wrong:

- Be amazing. TechCrunch will find you.

- Less is more. Know how to make your pitch in a sentence or two.

- Tell a compelling story.

- Be persistent. Once you've sent an e-mail to an individual editor (not all of them), a follow-up tweet the next day doesn't hurt.

- Keep e-mails really short, with bullet points of key stuff and a catchy/vision-oriented subject line.

- Explain the value proposition.

- Briefly mention team/competitive landscape if notable.

- Consider offering an exclusive.

QUORA

The most recent entry on my "must join" list is Quora, a rapidly growing question and answer site founded by two former Facebook veterans. What makes the site so useful for entrepreneurs is that (a) everyone must use his or her real name, and (b) an absolutely amazing number of world renowned venture capitalists, angel investors and entrepreneurs personally and thoughtfully answer questions posted from the community.

Here you will find answers direct from world-class investors, people such as Steve Case, Marc Andreessen, Fred Wilson, Keith Rabois, Mark Suster, Dave McClure, and many others. David S. Rose, the CEO of Gust and founder of New York Angels, has personally written an astounding 1,400 answers, most of which are on the topics of angel investing, venture capital and startups. And for those interested in strategic communications, my son and partner, Trace Cohen, has written dozens of answers on subjects including public relations, press release, and startup communications. Many of the answers on Quora get republished on websites such as Forbes, Huffington Post and Slate, but by signing up directly on Quora, you can join the conversation yourself, and access the fastest growing repository of current, useful information on thousands of subjects.

Own Your Venture Equity Simulator

D

Structuring relationships within the startup, calculating equity distribution, establishing valuation—these are among the most difficult steps in the evolution of every startup, and even minor mistakes can cause the startup to disintegrate. OwnYourVenture (http://www.ownyourventure.com) is a free equity simulator that you can use to simulate any number of "what if" scenarios involving the amount of investment, type and nature of investment, and resulting control. I recommend every startup work with OwnYourVenture to better understand the process.

The main benefit of OwnYourVenture is that it lets founders quickly understand how accepting different amounts of money in different ways will impact the ownership stake of the original owners. Some founders build elaborate spreadsheets for this purpose, but the OwnYourVenture equity simulator is much more visual.

Developed by OwnYourVenture, which advises entrepreneurs and early-stage companies, the equity simulator offers a user-friendly way to analyze how various deal terms impact the ownership of the company. On the left side of the screen are the "input" fields, such as the number of founders and premoney valuation (i.e., what the founders have put into the startup). The right column dynamically shows the results based on the input. In the center of the screen, a colorful pie chart visually summarizes the distribution of equity. As you make adjustments to inputs, you can quickly see how ownership shifts.

The equity simulator is especially useful because it forces founders to take into account the impact of future rounds of funding. Most founders are busy with the current round of funding and the details of running their companies. It's hard to think about funding requirements down the road. Yet most startups go through two or three rounds of funding, and founders are often surprised (not in a good way) about the cumulative impact on their ownership stakes.

The tool also guides founders to distinguish between two options that many startups fail to model correctly: convertible debt and down-round protection. This is not the place to get into the details of term sheets, but for now, convertible debt represents a loan to the company that is paid back in equity instead of cash. Being able to model the preferential price that angels use to calculate the payback amount is very useful to founders. When angels have down-round protection, if the startup goes down in value, angels have the right to be "made whole" on future financing rounds.

Most startups set aside some equity for key employees yet to be hired. The equity simulator has an "option pool" feature that allows startups to reserve a percentage of the equity for that purpose.

Let me emphasize that no simulator can take the place of competent legal or financial advice, but it is an excellent way to test different scenarios and plan accordingly. The equity simulator makes understanding the impact of raising money for an early-stage venture transparent and easy to grasp.

ACKNOWLEDGMENTS

We have many people to thank. Our deepest gratitude goes to David S. Rose, who took an abiding interest in our efforts and whose close-reading of the text made it even more responsive to the needs of entrepreneurs. We owe a debt to all the other members of the New York Angels and the entire New York City startup community for creating such a tight and supportive community for startups and investors. This is the community that collectively nurtured our entrepreneur dreams and now allows us to nurture others.

Before we thank a number of individuals who took time out of their busy lives to answer our relentless questions and review portions of our book, we'd be remiss not to acknowledge with gratitude our remarkable spouses. Carol Cohen, who married Brian, and Anna Beth Payne, who married John, are partners in every aspect of our lives and we are so indebted to them.

At McGraw-Hill, we would like to appreciate our editor Donya Dickerson, who immediately saw the merit in our proposal and helped guide the book to its present incarnation.

Thanks to all the investors and entrepreneurs who allowed us to add their hard-earned wisdom including Murat Aktihanoglu, Alain Bankier, Jeffrey Carr, Adam Dinow, Marissa Hermo, Linda Holliday, Scott Kurnit, Richard Laermer, Lily Liu, Phil Mark, Annette McClellan, Mike Michalowicz, Howard Morgan, Tom Patterson, Vanessa Pestritto, Jeff Pulver, Tucker

Robeson, John Sifonis, Ben Silbermann, David Steinberger, Gabriel Weinberg, Kyle Wild. Our book is infinitely richer for your advice and experience.

A number of institutions went of their way to assist us. First, our heartfelt thanks go to the Angel Capital Association for the education it has provided the investment community over the years.

Second, the New York City Economic Development Corporation merits applause for creating the wonderful startup environment that has put the Big Apple on the startup map. And we acknowledge both New York University and Columbia University for helping birth many of the companies mentioned in this book as well as thousands of other entrepreneurs.

This book would not have been possible without the indefatigable Anne Marie Rotondi, VP of Operations at Launch.it, whose attention to detail precisely compensates for the lack of our own.

Finally, we have a special shout-out for our children, all of whom in their own ways are pursuing the entrepreneur's path. We appreciate Trace Cohen, for cofounding Launch.it with his father. Nicole Cohen and Max Cohen are now creating their own entrepreneurial dreams that recognize new ways of looking at the world. Dan Kador, as cofounder of Keen IO, demonstrated to us that the lessons of this book really work. Rachel Kador supports entrepreneurs at digital agency Blue Fountain Media. We are indebted to them all.

INDEX

ABOUT THE AUTHORS

Brian Cohen is Chairman of the New York Angels, an independent consortium of individual accredited angel investors, providing seed and early-stage capital. Since 1997, members of NYA have invested more than $60 million in over 100 ventures. Brian deals with new product launches every day. Over the past decade, he estimates he has considered more than 1000 pitches for startups. He was the first investor in Pinterest. As an entrepreneur, Brian is building the first online content news release engagement launch platform for the PR industry. Launch. it is targeted to give entrepreneurs and companies of all sizes the opportunity to get quality visibility for their new products and ideas. Launch.it is now building relationships with major incubator and startup financing entrepreneur organizations to ensure their reach is as far-reaching and cost-effective as possible.

Brian and his wife, Carol, founded GlobalComm/TSI (Technology Solutions, Inc.). TSI was the first science and technology strategic marketing and public relations agency in New York. In 1996, TSI was recognized as the #1 fastest growing public relations agency in the U.S.

At TSI, Brian Cohen helped turn ordinary customers into fanatics on behalf of the companies his company represented. Major TSI clients included a 12-year partnership with Sony Corporation of America. For Sony, Brian helped launch over one hundred "bleeding-edge" products. For its alliance with IBM, Brian personally trained hundreds of IBM managers in media relations. As a testament to the success of this relationship, TSI received the Gold CIPRA award (#1 Public Relations program) in 1998 for the IBM Deep Blue/Gary Kasparov Chess Match concept development and public relations program. TSI was acquired by The McCann Erickson World Group, part of the Interpublic Group of Companies in 1997.

He developed Good Cause Communications, the first full-service not-for-profit PR firm designed to meet the needs of struggling non-profits. Its planned newswire, GoodCauseNews .org will be the first free newswire for struggling non-profits and PublicRelationsCares.com will be the first social responsibility volunteer program for public relations professionals.

Before launching TSI, Brian was a founding publisher of Computer Systems News and InformationWeek magazine at CMP Publications. While in graduate school, he was involved with pioneering computer trade publications including Personal Computing Magazine and Minicomputer News from Benwill Publishing.

Brian Cohen received two Honor B.S. degrees from Syracuse University in Biology and Speech Communications. He also received a Masters Degree in Science Communications from Boston University's School of Public Communications in 1978 and currently serves on the Dean's Advisory Board of Directors. He lives in New York City.

John Kador is the bestselling author of over 20 business books in the areas of leadership, careers, finance, and ethics. His most recent book is *Effective Apology: Mending Fences, Building Bridges, and Restoring Trust.*

His books for McGraw-Hill include the best-selling, *The Manager's Book of Questions: 751 Great Questions for Hiring the Best Person; 301 Best Questions to Ask On Your Interview;*

How to Ace the Brainteaser Job Interview; 50 High-Impact Speeches & Remarks: Proven Words You Can Adapt for Any Business Occasion; and *Net Ready: Strategies for Success in the E-conomy* (with Amir Hartman and John Sifonis).

John's other books include *Charles Schwab: How One Company Beat Wall Street and Reinvented the Brokerage Industry* and *Perfect Phrases for Writing Employee Surveys* (with Katherine Armstrong.

John assists leading CEOs in their own books, including *Pricing with Confidence: 10 Rules to Stop Leaving Money on the Table* by Reed Holden and Mark Burton; *The Six Sigma Leader* by Peter Pande; *The Manager's Book of Decencies: How Small Gestures Build Great Companies* by Steve Harrison; *A Call to Action: Taking Back Healthcare for Future Generations* by Henry McKinnell with John Kador; and *TechnoVision: The Executive's Guide for Understanding and Managing Information Technology* by Charles B. Wang.

John's writing practice also includes speechwriting, ghostwriting, and magazine journalism. He contributes to a number of leading business magazines and has columns in *Chief Executive*, *Registered Rep*, and *Human Resource Executive*.

He graduated from Duke University with a B.A. in English and received a masters degree in public relations from American University. He lives in Winfield, Pennsylvania, with his wife Anna Beth Payne. He has two children. Dan is working on a startup called Keen IO in San Francisco. Rachel works for Blue Fountain Media, a digital marketing agency in New York City.

For more information, visit John's website www.jkador.com.

ABOUT THE
NEW YORK ANGELS

The New York Angels is a member-led organization committed to finding, funding and mentoring great young companies
from pitch through a successful exit. Brian Cohen was named
Chairman in 2012, succeeding David S. Rose, Founder and
Chairman Emeritus.

The New York Angels is comprised of over 95 members.
Members are entrepreneurs, CEOs, venture capitalists and business leaders who have founded, funded and built world-class
companies. Angels come from a wide array of industry expertise
and together create an extensive network of entrepreneurial support. Angels mentor and coach the entrepreneurs in whom they
invest, serve on their boards, provide contacts, and assist with
team building, strategic planning and fundraising.

The mission of the New York Angels is to foster an engaged
and smart New York City angel investment environment in
an effort to enhance the opportunities for entrepreneurs to
be financed and succeed through exit. The New York Angels'
member mission is to provide opportunities for its members to
obtain outstanding financial returns by investing in early-stage
companies and accelerating them to market leadership. Angels
lead deals ranging from $100,000 to $1 million. The New York
Angels also works with a network of angel groups and venture

capital firms that it syndicates with to do deals up to $2 million. The New York Angels has been the leading seed investment organization in NYC for almost a decade, having invested over $60 million in more than 100 high-growth companies.

The New York Angels are the successor to the Angel Investor Program out of the New York New Media Association (NYNMA), a not-for-profit industry association founded in 1994 to support and promote the new media industry in the New York metro area. In 1997 the organization facilitated the creation of an Angel Investor Program to match promising entrepreneurs with experienced Angel Investors. By the time the Internet boom peaked, the NYNMA Angel Investors Program had provided more than $10 million in seed funding for over 30 new media companies.

In January, 2004, the Software & Information Industry Association (SIIA), the principal trade association for the software and digital content industry, took over the bulk of NYNMA's operating programs, and the active members of the NYNMA Angel Investors Program, under the leadership of David S. Rose, reformed the angel group as an independent investment organization with an expanded staff and more focused purview. In January of 2004, the 22 members of the former angel program, joined by a considerable number of fellow investors and with the blessing of SIIA, established the New York Angels, and re-dedicated themselves to vigorously investing in early-stage technology and new media companies in the New York City area and accelerating them to market leadership.

The New York Angels have made a personal and professional commitment to the ongoing development of the entrepreneurial ecosystem in New York City. This includes mentoring exciting local startup companies and lecturing and speaking on educational panels across the metropolitan area. It also includes deep relationships with the NYU Stern School of Business, Columbia Business School, Baruch College, Pace University, and the InSITE student counseling accelerator program. At these schools, New York Angel members participate in the annual business plan competition and also offer a "Future Angels" program for select business school students. Future Angels are carefully selected business school students who act as interns for the New York Angels. They get an opportunity to network with the Angels, attend meetings, and participate in due diligence. Additionally, the Angels work with the growing number of incubators in NYC.